CHERRY CREEK GOTHIC

UNIVERSITY OF OKLAHOMA PRESS : NORMAN

SANDRA DALLAS

CHERRY CREEK GOTHIC

VICTORIAN ARCHITECTURE IN DENVER

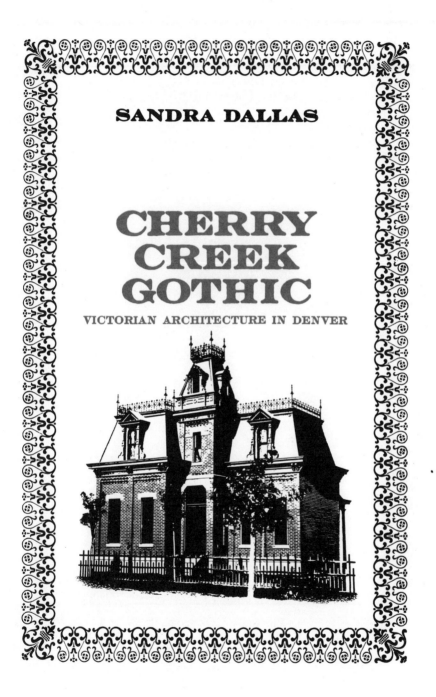

By SANDRA DALLAS

Gaslights and Gingerbread (Denver, 1965)

Gold and Gothic (Denver, 1967)

No More Than Five in a Bed: Colorado Hotels in the Old Days (Norman, 1967)

Vail (Boulder, 1969)

Cherry Creek Gothic: Victorian Architecture in Denver (Norman, 1971)

International Standard Book Number: 0–8061–0910–6

Library of Congress Catalog Card Number: 70–108801

Copyright 1971 by the University of Oklahoma Press, Publishing Division of the University. Composed and printed at Norman, Oklahoma, U.S.A., by the University of Oklahoma Press. First edition.

In Memory of
DONNA KAY DALLAS
Intrepid Explorer of Vacant Lots

PREFACE

WHEN I WAS EIGHT or thereabouts, my mother, like most conscientious mothers in those days, decided that I was to have the cultural advantages of piano lessons, and she dutifully led me to an imposing brick mansion on Grant Street and what she fervently hoped would be musical immortality. The lessons, despite the valiant efforts of my teacher and the exhortations of my mother to practice, resulted only in a few John Thompson melodies pounded out in atrocious rhythm (I never learned to count); but as a kind of side effect of the lessons, I discovered Grant Street architecture and historic Denver. I explored every foot of that old house, the Dennis Sheedy mansion at 1115 Grant, slinking along the halls covered with rubber mats, peering into the tiny marble sink with roses painted on its bowl in the back hall, going past the ponderous wooden doors up to the servants' quarters, where I always expected, half-fearfully, to see an ancient Pahaska (Buffalo Bill being my only experience with the Wild West at that time, not counting Roy Rogers) charge from a nook in the corridor. Even the bathroom was cause for awe; I had my first experience with a pull chain there.

I had an edge over my contemporaries of that post–World War II period because my parents realized the importance of imbuing me with a sense of Colorado's past; and while my friends were concentrating on kick-the-can, blissfully unaware of Larimer Street and Capitol Hill, Mother took my brother and me through the derelict halls of the Windsor Hotel, pointing out the diamond-dust mirrors and the bentwood chairs, even leading us firmly into the bar to see the holes Calamity Jane was supposed to have shot in the wall. (My brother, I recall, was infinitely more fascinated with the drunks.) It was only natural a few years later, when Duane Howell (a classmate and now photographer for the *Denver Post*) and I were writing an article for a college journalism class, that we chose the Windsor as our subject. One day shortly before the old hotel was torn down we wandered through the halls that once knew Oscar Wilde and Rudyard Kipling, H. A. W. Tabor and Robert Louis Stevenson. One of the pictures Duane took that day is included in these pages.

The Windsor is gone, and so are most of the Capitol Hill mansions that were familiar when I was growing up. The Sheedy house and a few like it, however, still stand, and I was reassured when I went into it not long ago—twenty years after I had first entered it with a music book clutched in my clammy hand—to see that little had changed. The mats on the hall floors still squeaked, along with the sound of the violins coming from behind formidable doors. The tapestry with the gold thread running through it still decorated the old servants' quarters, the tiny marble sink was in place, and I still expected to bump into some Pahaska-like figure.

This book, begun in the back halls of the Dennis Sheedy house, is the record of a twenty-five-year ramble through the city I love.

SANDRA DALLAS

Denver
April 11, 1971

ACKNOWLEDGMENTS

SINCE *Cherry Creek Gothic* is bits and pieces of public record and print garnered from innumerable sources, I am grateful to a number of people for helping me fit them together: Fred and Jo Mazzulla, generous friends who have shared their amazing collection of knowledge. The staff of the Denver Public Library, Western History Department—Mrs. Alys Freeze, Mrs. Opal Harber, Mrs. Mary Hanley, Mrs. Hazel Lundberg, and James H. Davis, whose interest in this project produced many a rare photograph. The staff of the State Historical Society of Colorado—Mrs. Enid T. Thompson, Mrs. Louisa Ward Arps, Mrs. Laura A. Ekstrom, and Mrs. Kay Pierson, who also spots pictures in unlikely places. And again, my thanks to Richard W. Purdie, who makes good photographs from bad.

SANDRA DALLAS

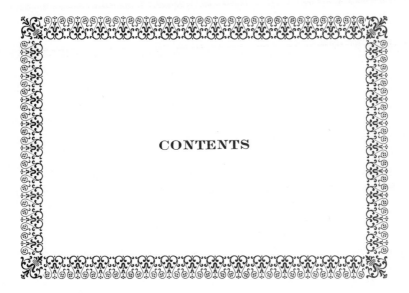

CONTENTS

	Preface	*page vii*
	Acknowledgments	*ix*
1.	The Founding Fathers	3
2.	Victoriana in Bloom	21
3.	Buffalo Tongue in Aspic	77
4.	Scratch Lane	119
5.	God's Country	161
6.	The Sporting Life	191
7.	. . . and Sporting Houses	227
8.	The Cherry Creek at Play	245
	Epilogue	277
	Bibliography	281
	Index of Structures	284
	Index	288
	Picture Map of Denver	22–23

CHERRY CREEK GOTHIC

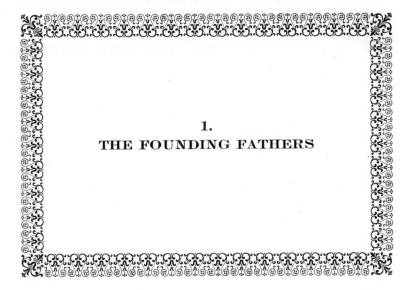

1.
THE FOUNDING FATHERS

When Green Russell—with a braided beard, a slouch hat, and a band of Georgia Crackers and Cherokee Indians—sloshed up the banks of the Cherry Creek to the point where it butts into the Platte River, he and his confreres pitched a couple of tents, piled a few logs together for a fire, and pulled out a collection of pans to begin working the streams for gold. That was the hurried founding of the town that would become Denver, Colorado. But far from emerging as Denver's first citizens, a distinction they cared little to claim, Green Russell and the boys were the first of a motley hodge-podge of gold-grubbers, gamblers, desperadoes, confidence men, prostitutes, and occasional decent souls who might in fact be called Denver's founding fathers.

Russell didn't take time to build more than a temporary shelter; as soon as he discovered Cherry Creek's gold was mostly mythical, he wandered away from the diggings to search in other spots. The men he left behind were only a little less impermanent; they built a sparse scattering of mud-plastered, cottonwood-joisted huts that gave the once pretty mountain-dropped valley a raw and ugly complexion. They uprooted the giant cottonwoods that banked the trickling Cherry Creek and, against the advice of the scavenging Utes who groveled about the camp, platted their towns to criss-cross the stream bottom. Cottonwood logs formed the frames of their cabins, chinked inside and out with river-wet clay. The doors and infrequent windows were covered with tanned skins or hewn logs roughly welded together. The floors were dirt and the roofs sod, which inspired the saw that rains generally continued inside three or four days after they had stopped outside.

The little settlement at the confluence of the Cherry Creek and the South Platte was given an ambitious lot of names that in 1860 succumbed to "Denver." The city originally was three different towns—Auraria on the west side of the Cherry Creek, St. Charles on the east side, and Denver City on top of St. Charles. The first structure in the first of the towns, Auraria, was a double log cabin thrown up on the east side of Eleventh Street between Wazee and Wynkoop in the early fall, 1858, by Green Russell, his brother, and an Indian trader named John Smith. The second was built a block away on Twelfth Street by Roswell Hutchins and John Easter. John Rooker erected the third, also on Twelfth Street, and A. H. Barker the fourth, at Twelfth and Wynkoop.

Auraria was already a thriving town when Charles Nichols crossed the creek and erected the first structure in what would become Denver City. Initially a log cabin with an unfinished roof, later a blacksmith shop, it was located at about Fourteenth and Blake. The Denver-side cabin was part of a town newly platted as St. Charles when General William H. Larimer arrived from Leaven-worth, spied the virtually unprotected townsite whose owners had hied it back to Kansas to register their claim, and jumped the claim. (It was inconsequential then or later that St. Charles–turned–Denver City was in Indian territory, so that neither group had a right to it.) The general moved into the unfinished Nichols cabin until his own was completed. The first building erected in the general's town, which he named "Denver" after the governor of

4

Kansas Territory—a point in his favor if the St. Charles men protested his acquisition of their townsite—was the general's own. Built by members of the "Leavenworth Party," it was one of four structures which marked the four corners of the intersection of Fifteenth and Larimer streets. The general's cabin, a rough, chinked-log structure, was on the southwest corner. Directly across Larimer was the Hickory Rogers cabin; diagonally across was a structure thrown up by two men named Lawrence and Dorsett; and across Fifteenth Street was the Moyne and Rice cabin, not only one of the first houses in Denver but also, if one wants to count a carpentry shop attached to it, Denver's first factory.

Larimer's cabin was luxurious, for the camp. He and his son Will moved into it in early December, 1858, and Larimer wrote his family:

> You have no idea how nice Will and I are fixed up. We have plenty of everything to eat. Today we had nice cakes, venison, beans, and molasses for dinner. We have a nice door with an old-fashioned wooden latch, with the string on the outside, of course. The fireplace, as is the custom in this country, is made of sods. In the southeast corner is the bunk; in the northwest corner the window, four panes of glass with sash. On the north side, between the end of the bed and the fireplace, we have two shelves and a bench, all made with a nice slab. We cut the meat on the bench and set water buckets on the other two shelves . . . . On the northeast side and corner we hang our coats, guns, and things. I have a nail box, shovels, and old boots and buffalo overshoes under the bunk . . . . I am writing on a nice pine table under the window, covered with the gray horse blanket as nice as the day we started. . . . I have David Copperfield, my Bible, and your Prayer Book, together with some old newspapers and a lot of Mr. Collier's books on this table . . . . You have no idea how comfortable we all live. We sleep warm and nice.

The general had not yet begun to read Mr. Collier's books when Charles H. Blake and Andrew J. Williams arrived from Crescent City, Iowa, threw up a big tent, and opened Denver's first mercantile business. By December 1, 1858, they had erected a large double cabin to hold their merchandise, Denver's first store. Hardly had

Blake and Williams settled down to enjoy their monopoly when two other merchants, Kinna and Nye, showed up with a load of hardware, sheet iron, tinner's goods, and supplies to open up competition. A few days later J. D. Ramage opened the first jewelry shop in a log cabin in Auraria, despite the fact that business must have been poor, since there was little money in the town to spend for jewelry and few women to spend it on. A couple of weeks later, on Christmas Eve, Richens L. ("Uncle Dick") Wootton pulled in from New Mexico with a wagonload of Taos lightning, prime rot-gut, to liven the holiday spirit. He erected the first two-story cabin in the settlement, ambitiously known as the first business block, on the Cherry Creek bottom, 1413–15 Eleventh Street. For all its importance as the town's main meeting hall, the "Wootton Block" was a dingy log building with a sloped-roof attic lighted by a four-pane glass window. Uncle Dick lined up empty kegs to serve as a counter and operated the business as a combined saloon, store, and public auditorium. "There wasn't much money in town," he once remarked, "but I got most of what there was." Prosperity was short-lived for Uncle Dick, however; he was generally known as a soft touch.

Nearly as important to the settlement as the saloon on the first floor of Uncle Dick's building was the newspaper started on the second. William N. Byers, newly arrived from Omaha with wagon full of type and some journalistic notions, rented Uncle Dick's attic and put out the Cherry Creek's first newspaper, the *Rocky Mountain News*. While dodging the rain that came through the roof and the bullets that came through the floor, Byers managed to put out Denver's first paper April 23, 1859, beating a competitor by a couple of hours. As the leader of Denver's fourth estate— indeed, as its only member—Byers soon sought other quarters, and the upstairs room was turned into a gambling den.

Businesses came quickly to the little town that had no reason for being there. There was no gold in the Cherry Creek, so Denver rationalized its existence by becoming a supply point. The second saloon was opened by Rice and Heffner at Eleventh and Market Streets in January, 1859. Tom Pollock began the settlement's first

6

smithy, probably in the half-finished Charles Nichols cabin on the Denver side of the creek, January 10, 1859. John Ming opened a grocery store a few days later.

Davide Smoke, Count Henri Murat (a ubiquitous little man who claimed kinship with Joachim Murat, former king of Naples), and Henri's squat frau Katrina opened the diggings' first hotel, a stumpy, mud-plastered timber cabin with a flat roof and an earth floor, homemade furniture, and buffalo-robe beds. While Smoke did the menial tasks about the shanty they slyly named the "Eldorado" and Katrina scrubbed and cooked and ripped up her best red flannel petticoat to make the settlement's first American flag, the count mounted the log tower that squatted like a fat cupola on top of the roof to scan the horizon for wagon trains. When he spotted one, he would bolt from the roof and rush out to greet it, barking the virtues of his modest hostelry. Never very successful with any of his short-lived business ventures, Murat gave his partner a quitclaim on the Eldorado in April, 1859, only two months after they had opened it, and moved to the Denver side of the creek, where he engaged in the baking business. By June he had given that up too, and opened a barbershop at 1426 Larimer. Murat gained his lasting fame in the barbershop, where he demanded one dollar for shaving Horace Greeley, who was visiting the Cherry Creek to report on gold discoveries to his *New York Tribune* readers. Katrina charged three dollars to launder half a dozen pieces of Greeley's linen, and the exorbitant fees caused Greeley to remark wryly that there was at least one man in the camp determined to make the best of his opportunities. But determined though he might have been, Murat was a failure. He attempted an incredible number of ventures in Denver, but none met with what one could call success. The count died in the early 1890's, and Katrina lived on for another twenty years on the charity of the Pioneer Ladies Aid Society by claiming she was the first white woman in the Cherry Creek Diggings (which she wasn't).

A few doors from where Murat gave dollar shaves, George Wakely opened the first photographic studio at 1440 Larimer, advertising pictures printed on leather to send to the folks back home. Across the street from him, at 1425 Larimer, Libeus Barney built Apollo Hall, where Denver's first theater troupe performed. The following summer George W. Brown and his brother Samuel opened Denver's first bank, at 1429 Larimer, a struggling affair in a flimsy shack. It lasted only a short time. A month or so after the Browns opened their bank, Milton E. Clark, Austin M. Clark, and E. Henry Gruber started Denver's first mint. The partners had begun construction of their two-story brick and stone building at Sixteenth and Market in the spring of 1860, and on July 20 they minted their impressive first coins. "Clark, Gruber & Co." was stamped on one side and "Pikes Peak Gold" on the other. The first "mint drops" were pure gold but so soft that Clark, Gruber had to begin using the same alloy as the United States, except that the Denver mint used 1 per cent more gold. The U.S. government purchased Clark, Gruber in 1863 for $25,000 and a sales agreement that Denver would get a federal mint. Instead the Treasury Department used the Clark, Gruber building as a gold-buying office, and Denver didn't get its mint until 1905.

Another first that caused a great commotion in the combined cities was the founding of the diggings' first school—in Auraria on the west side of Twelfth Street. Accustomed to taking its citizens' peculiarities in stride, Denver nevertheless was shocked at its first schoolmaster, Professor Owen J. Goldrick, who arrived to begin his teaching duties dressed in a glossy plug hat, broadcloth Prince Albert, boiled shirt, and pastel gloves, cracking a bullwhip over his team of oxen as he swore at them in Latin. The honorable mutton-chop-whiskered professor was a student of ancient languages, orthography, philosophy, science, English grammar, and cheap whisky (which probably killed him, but only after he had had flamboyant careers as schoolmaster, journalist, and editor).

By the summer of 1859, the settlement on the Cherry Creek had an impressive catalogue of businesses. According to an ambitious local promotion booklet, *Denver City and Auraria, the Commercial Emporium of the Pike's Peak Gold Regions in 1859*, the town boasted 420 structures (250 frame, 150 log, 20 brick, a few being adobe) and three thousand permanent residents. Under

8

occupations, the booklet listed bakers, barbers, book-sellers, carpenters, druggists, engineers, hotelkeepers, merchants, physicians, real estate agents, saloonkeepers, watchmakers, and jewelers.

Other accounts of the early city in "this country of premature fame and undeserved celebrity" were less than enthusiastic. Libeus Barney estimated that there were two hundred log houses and six frame ones under construction. Early-day travel editor Albert Dean Richardson gave the same disparaging view of Denver in his book *Beyond the Mississippi*. Almost all of the three hundred buildings, he estimated, were made of hewn logs, and nearly a third of them, erected during the winter on speculation, were unfinished and roofless. Very few had glass windows or doors, and only two or three sported board floors. One enterprising lady, in a moment of abandon, sewed together corn sacks for a carpet and covered her walls with sheets and tablecloths to give her home a decided air of luxury. Inside, the cabins were fitted with adobe hearths and fireplaces; chimneys were made of sticks of wood "piled up like children's cob-houses" and plastered with mud. The furnishings consisted of stools, tables, pole beds, and rough boxes for dressers. Chairs were rare.

Richardson and a couple of friends—one of them Horace Greeley, who had snubbed the town's best hotel—jumped a deserted cabin and moved in. The new residents found themselves in a lavishly furnished cottage that had a chair of elders fresh from the forest with the bark still on, and a rare luxury—a mattress. The cabin had no window, only a door, with wooden hinges, that opened not with a key but with a penknife. A few days after Richardson and Greeley acquired the cabin, its owner came home unexpectedly, according to Richardson, "but observing that the nine points of the law were in our favor, he apologized humbly for his intrusion (most obsequious and marvelous of landlords!) begged us to make ourselves entirely at home, and then withdrew, to jump the best vacant cabin *he* could find."

Despite its seeming affluence and its large number of businesses, Denver had a noticeable scarcity of one type of establishment—the brothel. There were few prostitutes in Denver (although a miner could visit one of the tipis on the Platte and purchase the favors of an Indian woman for a nominal fee paid to her husband) and even fewer bawdyhouses. What the town lacked in one kind of sporting house, however, was generously made up for in other kinds. Gambling halls, billiard parlors, and saloons were thickly clustered along the muddy streets and occasional board sidewalks. Libeus Barney, who was at the time erecting his own saloon and gaming house, noted disdainfully that every third building was a groggery "dealing out whiskey at from 10 to 20 cents a 'nip' and warranted to kill at fifty yards." Another imbiber estimated every fifth house to be a bar, a whisky shop, or a lager-beer saloon, and every tenth a gambling house, whereas a third noted that along Blake Street liquor stores and saloons were behind almost every door. The quantity, however, was unimportant; it was the quality of the saloons that mattered, and this was generally iniquitous—from the most modest wine shop to that "king hell-hole of the consolidated city," the Denver House, later notorious as the Elephant Corral, where up to eight hundred gold-seekers would crowd in during a single night to lap up the liquor and attempt to buck the tiger.

By March, 1860, Denver boasted a number of business streets lined with a variety of enterprises. Along Blake, the city's principal street, were the Denver House, a blacksmith shop run by a Parisian, the store of a Jewish merchant who advertised "White, Red, and Orange Flannels," a Vienna bakery, a drugstore, the Pike's Peak stage office, a chair factory, and Jones and Cartwright, a supply store carrying groceries (sugar, crackers, coffee, molasses, mackerel, and herring), rope, blasting powder, nails, boots, locks, hatchets, and screws, all of which the dealers would "sell low for cash."

On McGaa Street, later notorious as Holladay, Denver's red-light line, were the Exchange Coffee House, a livery stable, reading rooms, a large block of stores, and a room "occupied as a drinking and billiard saloon by American citizens of African descent." On the next street, Larimer, were a theater, Simm's Eating House and Billiard Saloon, and the Broadwell House (the first completely finished frame building in the city). Lawrence Street hosted the

The first building erected in the Cherry Creek Diggings. The couple pictured in the drawing probably are Indian trader John Smith and his Indian wife, who undoubtedly preferred the tipi to the cabin (*Denver Public Library Western Collection*).

General William H. Larimer's cabin, where the Granite Hotel stands today. General Larimer himself may be the man in this 1858 lantern slide (*Denver Public Library Western Collection*).

The first two-story building in Denver, the Wootton Block, whose attic was the first home of the *Rocky Mountain News* (*Denver Public Library Western Collection*).

powder magazine, several Indian-trader stores, Denver's finest Gothic-style cottage, and both the Methodist Church and the city's first brothel. Way out on Arapahoe were half a dozen cabins and two or three frame cottages. Except for a few mud-chinked cabins and Indian tipis farther out, that was Denver City.

The "Eldorado," the first hotel at the Cherry Creek, is pictured in this painting by Herndon Davis (1941). Flying from the tower is the flag, the first in the settlement, made from Mrs. Murat's petticoat. The building was discovered in 1939 under the siding of an old house at 1249 Tenth Street. It was purchased by May Bonfils Stanton and moved to the Stanton estate on Wadsworth Boulevard, where it stands today (*Denver Public Library Western Collection*).

Denver continued to grow in ungainly jumps, spreading along the Cherry Creek and the South Platte, across the prairies back toward Leavenworth, and west to the range known as the Shining Mountains. Its barren plains-town look came from its scattering of board buildings—sometimes painted, more often not—and an equal number of hewn-log shacks, all surrounded by scraggly trees and chicken-scratched yards. Occasionally someone threw up a

The fourth location of the *News* was in this plush frame building, constructed on pilings in the Cherry Creek bed. Editor William N. Byers chose the spot for his press because it was neutral territory between Denver and Auraria. The building was swept away in the 1864 flood, and parts of the paper's presses were found scattered miles downstream (*Denver Public Library Western Collection.*)

brick building, but not very often; cheap, hastily built wooden structures were far more common, and far more susceptible to fire.

Despite the lamentable shortage of fire-fighting equipment and trained units of men, early settlers were incredibly nonchalant about fire, and Colorado history is ablaze with conflagrations. Denver's great fire broke out early on the morning of April 19, 1863, in the rear of the Cherokee House, a nondescript hotel at

Shown on a busy day is the interior of the *Rocky Mountain News* building on the Cherry Creek bottoms. The street floor was the editorial and press room, the basement was a storeroom and job-printing department, and the attic was used as sleeping quarters by the printers.

the corner of Fifteenth and Blake, known in history only for its part in the fire. A steady wind fanned the flames that burned the heart of the city's business district in two hours, reducing the best part of Denver to a charred mass with only an occasional blackened fireproof building left standing. Along the trickle of the Cherry Creek lay a motley smattering of belongings hastily rescued from the burning buildings. With a spirit born of frontier settlement, however, Denver began to rebuild on the warm ashes, but with a noticeable change—combustible pitch-pine buildings were outlawed. Unique among Western cities, Denver was to be almost entirely brick-built.

Scarcely had the burned-out buildings been replaced when

This group in front of the Holladay Overland Mail & Express Co., corner of Fifteenth and Market, is waiting for the stage to arrive. Ben Holladay, an enterprising businessman, purchased the Overland Stage Line in 1862 for $700,000 and sold it four years later to Wells, Fargo for $1.8 million. Early Market was known first as McGaa, then as Holladay Street, until Ben's friends complained that it wasn't proper to call the city's most notorious red-light street by the name of an early pioneer (*Denver Public Library Western Collection*).

Denver's savage 1864 flood swept away on its first wave the *Rocky Mountain News,* and printers sleeping in its loft barely had time to escape. Parts of the *News*'s presses were found for miles downstream; remnants of the Washington hand press used to print the first issue were found thirty-five years later buried in the stream bed under a dozen feet of sand (*Library, State Historical Society of Colorado*).

Denver was hit by a second disaster—a flood that swooped down the Cherry Creek destroying the section of the city that lined the stream. Indians had warned the first settlers about building on the Cherry Creek bottoms, but nobody had paid them much heed; it was inconceivable that the trickling creek could grow to flood proportions. Early one morning in May, 1864, however, the Cherry Creek, swollen by heavy rains, went on the rampage. Raging like the wrath of God, it ravished buildings, uprooted trees, and swallowed blocks of buildings in its path; and in its wake was left a trail of destruction as wide as the charred mess from the fire the year

17

before. The swollen waters and the flames of the 1863 blaze destroyed almost all of the early city. The Denver that emerged from the ruins, divested of its dirty petticoats and dressed in the wealth beginning to flow from the mountains, was to become in garb and garishness the Queen City of the Plains.

On the wave of prosperity that hit Denver in the mid–1860's came a lust for lavish living that culminated in an extravagant building boom that made of the city a remarkable hodge-podge of coy Victorian styles. The new Denver was a plumed peacock, happily gilded in frontier falderal. Gone were the Blake Street shanties and the Platte Valley soddies, and in their places, by city ordinance, rose palaces of brick, top-heavy with corbeling, haughty with pillars, pretentious with plate-glass windows. To prevent another conflagration, the city council passed a law requiring all business buildings in downtown Denver to be erected of brick or stone, and one by one the flimsy, false-fronted wood cabins were replaced with substantial brick blocks and stone castles.

Governor John Evans complained in 1863 when he built his home that there was not a building in Denver that boasted a spire. A year later the Denver skyline was mutilated with steeples and cupolas with mansard roofs, crenelated walls, Italian towers, and Gothic spires that nosed their way above the fledgling trees planted in hopes they could turn the chicken yards into rusticated Roman bowers, instant ruins, "pleasing decay."

"The distinguishing charm of Denver architecture," wrote a contemporary, "is its endless variety. Almost every citizen is laudably ambitious to build a house unlike that of his neighbor, and is more desirous that it shall have some novel feature than that it shall be surpassingly beautiful." Scorning architectural purity, Denver's early builders put together Victorian styles in every possible combination with a naïvety that produced Greek revivals with mansard roofs and Gothic castles with Italian tops. Then they trimmed everything with that imaginative creation of the Victorian era, cast iron. Framing every Denver house was a lacy iron fence, its lines frozen in concentric circles, heart-shaped loops, mock spears, heavy ropes, and intricate curves. The flat-top houses were

18

These picnickers, standing far out on the prairie at about Sixteenth and Sherman, view a Denver that rose from the ravages of the 1863 fire and the 1864 flood a city of Victorian splendor. Only two years after the flood, the spreading settlement was beginning to show Gothic churches and Italianate homes (*Library, State Historical Society of Colorado*).

crowned with lace-like lines or cast-iron flower chains; the mansard sloping sides were outlined with rows of iron daggers. Cast-iron deer regarded formal gardens in metallic silence as streams of water, shot from tiered iron fountains, played in the air.

This architecture, the styles of which were easily identifiable although combined with each other, gave a charm and a certain character to the *nouveau riche* frontier town. The buildings sprouted from a doubtful Italian design—a slicked-off roof with dripping trim and round-top windows. Or they bloomed from Gothic roots planted in the preflood era. Or they flowered along the shaded streets of California and Arapahoe, Curtis and Welton, in mansardic styles which had appeared only occasionally a few years before.

Nearly every building erected after the flood boasted a Victorian detail—from a modest "out-back" with a carpenter-Gothic bargeboard to the spectacular Tabor Grand Opera House with its brutal Renaissance trim. The periods were seldom secularized; they were mixed with abandon, comingled without restraint, dumped into an architectural caldron that spewed out a style so distinct, an "exterior decoration" so decidely Denver, that it emerged with a name of its own—Cherry Creek Gothic.

2.
VICTORIANA IN BLOOM

GOTHIC was the first architectural style to come to the Cherry Creek. Denver wasn't yet a year old when Dick Whitsitt, real estate agent and original member of General Larimer's party, put up a frame Gothic cottage on the outskirts of Denver on Lawrence Street. Before the fire, one could find here and there traces of carving, buds of spires and cupolas, and occasional attempts at fretwork porches or decorated gables. But the pretentions were timid until the mid–1860's when Denver was suddenly transformed from an infant settlement into a grown-up Victorian city.

Simple Greek-style architecture was passé when Denver was built; Gothic, a massive style copied after the cathedrals of Europe, had lines that translated surprisingly well into wood—the cathedral high-arched windows, the sharp gables filled in with carved cross bars and fretted bargeboards, the vertical board-and-battens. Gothic had been a particularly fitting style for churches because of its upward lines, its spires and elevated arches, all pointing the

"Denver Bird's Eye View, 1892" (*Library, State Historical Society of Colorado*).

way to heaven, but, of course, this was not the reason the Victorian settlers of Denver liked it; they liked it because it was stylish, and because it was decorative. It lent itself easily to "carpenter Gothic," a fanciful, scroll-sawn, design-heavy style, which later, built in stone again, became splendid Capitol Hill mansions.

Equally as popular as Gothic was Italianate, whose features—towers, flat roofs, loggias, and that all-time Victorian favorite the cupola—were generally weakened by trim in other styles. Corniced with a bracketed design, the Italian was a popular style for stores too crowded together to afford Gothic spires and prominent archways; the round-head windows—often emphasized by raised keystones or artfully decorated crowns—and the trimmed flat roof, however, gave a fashionable look to an otherwise ordinary building. The Italian villa-like style was particularly suited for residences, where its basic features produced modish, formal houses that could be decorated further by Gothic or Oriental or mansardic details.

Another style the Denver Victorians held dear—not for its own lines but for its adaptability—was the mansard. Originally designed by a man named Mansard to utilize waste attic space, the gently sloping roof, flat on top, had great charm, whether it was broken by protruding gables, used by itself on the top of a cupola, or combined with the more prosaic Gothic roof. The mansard was never used as a pure style; indeed, it was not a house design at all but merely a roof.

Like American Victorians all over the country, Denverites were far too sophisticated to limit their house designs to a simple one or two. They reached back into the past to garner the features of any period they could adapt to their buildings, particularly their houses —and a few they couldn't. Gothic, Italianate, mansard, Romanesque, Greek, Moorish, Oriental—even Platte River soddy—were the components of Denver's unique architecture.

When Governor John Evans built his fashionable home on the desolate prairie at Fourteenth and Arapahoe, all Denver thought him mad. Alone and so far out on the plains, he would likely be attacked by Indians. It wasn't long before Denver caught up with

By the time of the 1864 flood, Denver was just beginning to show a collection of smart Gothic cottages with cathedral windows and sharp gables, their harsh lines occasionally being softened by carved barge-boards and spindly porches. These simple houses at Fifteenth and Arapahoe—with a choice of back houses—were soon torn down to be replaced by Denver's first full-bloom Victorian homes (*Library, State Historical Society of Colorado*).

him, however, and made his home the focal point of the city's first upper-crust neighborhood.

Denver City was still a raw settlement when it began dividing itself into "good" and "bad" neighborhoods. The closer a house stood to the Indian tipis on the Platte, the poorer the area; the farther east, the more fashionable. Denver's early suburbs spread out from the city core like the fingers of a hand—southwest from Auraria, north and east along Welton, Arapahoe, Stout, and west to the Highlands. Neighborhoods sprang into being—University

25

A simple combination of styles in the 1700 block of Pennsylvania—a carpenter Gothic house with Gothic gable, Italian windows, and Greek fret design.

Although she probably never met Eugene Field when he was a Denver newspaperman in the early 1880's the unsinkable Mrs. J. J. Brown, with an aplomb he would have applauded, claimed they were confidants and spearheaded a drive to save Field's Denver house, 315 West Colfax, when it was threatened with demolition. Largely because of Maggie's efforts, the tiny Gothic-style house was moved from its downtown location to Washington Park, where for years it served as a public library.

Park, Globeville, Montclair, Argo, and Barnum (named for the famous showman who found himself the sucker at his own game when he invested in Colorado real estate). But all these were slackers compared to the plush area that grew up around the Evans home. Bordered roughly by Lawrence and Welton, the section began at the Cherry Creek and faded into a pleasant middle-class area close to Twentieth. The massive mansions of the 1870's and

27

Modern architects gasp at the proportions used by Victorian designers, but few buildings built today have the jaunty air of this house that stood at Clarkson and Park Avenue with its pretentious mansarded cupola and lace-work crown.

1880's were clustered around Fourteenth and Arapahoe. A decidedly Victorian bunch—with their obvious mansard roofs, cathedral spires, and Gothic gables—they were architectural triumphs of unknown designers who catered to the *nouveaux riches*, whose tastes were not yet sophisticated from world travel.

Typical of the mansard style which sometimes made the house all roof was the home of Wolfe Londoner, Denver grocer and mayor, at 2222 Champa. A small structure razed in 1940, the house appeared larger because of the sloping lines of the roof.

One of the delights of the mansard was the ease with which it could be combined with other styles, an obvious advantage to the Victorians. Here the mansard, decidedly out of proportion on this Grant Street house, is crushed under a hip roof.

Next door to the Baptist Church at Seventeenth and Stout stood this impressive mansarded house belonging to Charles Chever (*Denver Public Library Western Collection*).

Little children would have run in terror from this place a few years after this picture was taken. The house was erected by W. B. Daniels, scion of Daniels, Fisher & Co. Later the house at Fourteenth and Curtis became the Inter-Ocean gambling club (*Denver Public Library Western Collection*).

The John B. Hindry family built this Italian-style residence at 5500 North Washington. Long considered a haunted house by neighborhood children, it frightens no one anymore; it is gone (*Denver Public Library Western Collection*).

An imaginative delight for some Denver Victorian—an Italian pagoda. (*Denver Public Library Western Collection*).

Far from unique, 1255 Tremont, nevertheless drew artists and sight-seers because of its incongruous setting in the midst of downtown Denver and because most people don't know where to find the city's Victorian architecture.

Italian architecture is apparent in the detail of this villa-like house, 2504 Champa.

There was nothing more appealing to the Victorians than a combination of art and ingenuity; they loved cast iron. Not only could they use every imaginable design to produce intricate embellishments for their homes, but mass production made cast iron an inexpensive adornment. Cast-iron scrolls and circles, daggers and spears, rickrack and lacework were used for gates, fences, roof crowns, fountains, furniture, and garden statues. It was a dowdy house indeed that lacked a bit of cast-iron lace lovingly placed in a conspicuous spot.

The J. W. Iliff home was an iron-foundry dream—having a cast-iron fence around the house, another on top of the roof, iron balconies and railings and porch pillars, iron hitching posts and street lamp, cast-iron spires on the carriage house, and a tiered cast-iron fountain in the yard.

Many of the following drawings are from an 1880 *History of Denver*, which featured thirty views of Denver's finest homes. Not one of them stands today.

The John Evans house, first of the fashionable residences in the city's first upper-class neighborhood, was a red-brick mansion trimmed in white, originally one and a half stories, later enlarged to three. The house stood at the corner of Fourteenth and Arapahoe, and the lawn stretched to the Cherry Creek. Both private home and governor's mansion, the house was visited by President Ulysses S. Grant and a host of generals and statesmen.

John Evans' son, William Gray Evans, lived in this fine house at Thirteenth and Bannock, built by *Rocky Mountain News* editor William N. Byers. Shrouded in trees today, it is still occupied by an Evans (*Denver Public Library Western Collection*).

There was as much money—sometimes more—in supplying the needs of the mining men as in discovering the mines. Nathaniel P. Hill, a brilliant young engineer, built the first smelter in the Rocky Mountains at Black Hawk, then others at Alma and Argo, near Denver, and made a fortune. Part of it he put into one of the Cherry Creek's first castles, a French château at Fourteenth and Welton. In the handsome mansion with its cathedral spire and chimneys like triumphal arches the Hills began a tradition of social entertaining that reached its peak when their son's wife, Mrs. Crawford Hill, became the undisputed leader of Denver society.

Despite the fact that his heart was in the Colorado ranchlands, Joseph P. Farmer managed to hold his own in Denver society with this modest cottage at Eighteenth and Arapahoe. A cattleman with extensive holdings throughout Colorado, Farmer maintained this Italian-style residence in Denver, with a spacious carriage house to shelter a few of his 150 horses.

David H. Moffat's impressive home at Fourteenth and Curtis was only a forerunner of the mansion he later built on Capitol Hill. A banker and railroader, Moffat built a large, shuttered home complete with two Victorian favorites, a cupola and a secluded love seat, although it is doubtful that the trees newly planted on the prairie were tall enough to give any privacy. A few years after this picture was drawn, the home became an elegant boardinghouse for fifty of Denver's most prominent young bachelors.

3031 Curtis (gone)

Because Denver grew up at the height of the Victorian era, it was one of the most Victorian cities in the country. Many residents feel that the nineteenth-century aspect of the city was razed along with the pretentious buildings on Capitol Hill; few people are aware that within walking distance of downtown Denver lies a Victorian neighborhood almost completely intact. Gothic, Italian, mansardic—nearly every style of nineteenth-century architecture is used in these houses. Never Denver's plushest area, the neighborhood was a respectable middle-class section filled with proper little houses. Only a few stores and apartment buildings were built there originally, and unlike most of Denver's older areas, this section

45

2747 Champa

46

2810 Curtis

2445 California in 1888, the George W. Kramer home. It still stands, structurally the same but seedy with age (*Denver Public Library Western Collection*).

never became commercial; it never became a warehouse area or factory center. Roughly bounded by Twenty-sixth and Thirtieth streets, Lawrence and California, this neighborhood at the edge of the Skyline Urban Renewal project lies in a semislum trance waiting to be torn down or perhaps discovered by someone with the money and imagination to clean it up and turn it into one of the finest Victorian restorations in the country.

When the elegant mansions on Fourteenth and Arapahoe and Welton and Lawrence began to get seedy and give way to commercial enterprises, Denver society looked for a new place to settle. South and north were the middle-class areas, west—well, a lady had

2425–27 Champa (gone)

2625 California

to cross the railroad tracks to get to town. East was Brown's Bluff, acres of prime prairie land just waiting to be settled. Henry C. Brown had homesteaded the land east of Broadway and once attempted to rid himself of the property for a greedy $500. But the buyer backed down before the deal was completed, saying the land never would be worth the price, and Brown changed his mind, remarking that the land might make him rich. Dutifully, he laid out dirt streets, named for presidents and generals—Lincoln, Sherman, Grant, Logan—platted his old homestead, and turned it into the wealthiest subdivision Denver ever saw.

Gambler Ed Chase built an impressively Victorian mansion for his third bride, a Palace chorine. Located at 2859 Lawrence, the house, now gone, was drawn nearly thirty years ago by painter Herndon Davis for a series of newspaper articles on old Denver. Chase later moved to 1492 Race, and after his death his widow sold that property to the Aladdin Theatre (*Denver Public Library Western Collection*).

The city's society, recently returned from innumerable enlightening trips to Europe, was ripe for Henry's hawkers with their plots of land suitable for prairie castles. Massive stone citadels, towered and turreted, guarded by stone lions, surrounded by lance-like fences, sprang up where only a few years before Indian tipis had squatted. Inside these preposterous mansions were tapestried walls, polished woods, crystal chandeliers, and jewellike windows. Henry C. Brown was right; his old homestead did make him rich.

The first of the stone castles to rise on the barren prairie, whose name had only recently been changed from Brown's Bluff to Capitol Hill, was built by Harold B. Kountze, a member of the spectacular Denver banking family which organized the Colorado National Bank. Called "the fortress" for its tremendous size, the mansion featured a heat plant (located in the stables) which shot hot air into the house through a huge tunnel, and two-foot-thick brick and stone walls, reportedly designed to protect the family from Indians, although the builder claimed their real purpose was temperature and sound control. The walls may have held off savages, but they couldn't withstand the wrecker's ball, which razed them several years ago to make way for a life insurance building.

One by one the castles rose on the barren prairie, so far from the rest of Denver that the mistress of one lamented that only her friends with carriages could visit her. Most of them are gone now— the Richard B. Pearce house at 1712 Sherman, a brick and stone and half-timbered home where Central City's Cornish miners gathered, and the white stone mansion with five parlors, two dining rooms, and gold doorplates built at Eighth and Logan by John Campion. Gone, too, is the magnificent French château and Romanesque castle built by William Church on Quality Hill, an eastward extension of Capitol Hill. Fitted with a rare red-birch lavishly carved Moorish fireplace, tooled leather walls, a massive stairway whose landing held a twelve-foot pull-out stage, and French crystal windows, the "Church Castle," which architects and historians alike insisted should be preserved as a museum, was torn down several years ago to make way for an apartment building.

A few of the prairie castles still stand, however, enduring precarious existences when once they knew grand balls, lavish dinners, political and social intrigues—Croke's sandstone palace, Moffat's manor, and that garish work of art and architecture, Maggie Brown's House of Lions.

There was something suspicious about people who chose to live in apartments. At a time when the apex of social accomplishment

52

Standing like a squat
sentinel on the prairie,
this cornerstone is all that
remains of a vanished
castle at the corner
of Seventeenth and
Sherman.

Victoriana in bloom, from *Souvenir Album of Denver*, 1890 (*Library, State Historical Society of Colorado*).

It wasn't that William Garret Fisher, one of the owners of Daniels & Fisher, a department store, had less money than the other Capitol Hill millionaires; he just had more taste. His home, a marvel of simplicity in that neighborhood of unrelieved stone castles and French châteaux, was American colonial style, built of polished lava stone with Grecian columns and only occasional carvings. Inside, although simple in comparison, the house conformed more to the standards of Logan Street with a third-floor drawing room and halls finished in bird's-eye maple and rosewood. When Fisher added a $75,000 art gallery and ballroom with a stage large enough to accommodate a full-size orchestra a few years after the house was built, just for his daughter's wedding, his neighbors decided he wasn't so eccentric after all.

Typical of the mansions that lined Grant Street ("millionaires row") in almost unrelieved monotony was cattleman Dennis Sheedy's red-brick sandstone-trimmed home. With its sharp Gothic gables, expansive pillared porch, and assortment of towers, loggias, and window sizes and shapes, the Sheedy home, 1115 Grant, was a prime example of Grant Street Gothic. Today the old home is a fine arts conservatory, and its stairways, covered by rubber pads, are trod by music students; the paneled walls, covered in tapestry and goat hide, absorb the sounds of instruments; and the sliding doors open onto prosaic lesson rooms.

was a house on Capitol Hill and everything else was just a step in that direction, apartment dwelling was something Denver people didn't understand. Even a tiny cottage with only an iron-picket fence was preferable to living with a lot of strangers. For the most part Denver residents weren't sophisticated enough to think of apartments as fashionable flats or to appreciate them for their convenience (which never was popular with the Victorians any-

Most of the residents of Capitol Hill were content to employ Gothic or French or Romanesque—or a combination of all three—in their baronial mansions, devoting only a room or two to such less fashionable styles as Egyptian or Moorish. So it was a radical departure when Indian-fighter Hal Sayre, surveyor and mining man, used the Alhambra as the model for his Logan Street home. Having scalloped cherrywood arches and lavishly decorated turquoise borders about the windows, the house was Sayre's pride and ranked in his esteem only with the Indian scalp he had taken at Sand Creek. Next door to the massive Moffat mansion, Sayre's Alhambra today is a home for working girls.

way). Apartments always had the taint of tenements about them; they were only a step removed from living above the store.

Denver, nevertheless, did provide a few apartment units for those who bucked popular sentiment and chose to live in them. And as if to make up for their unpopularity, these buildings were

Nobody took the mandate that a Capitol Hill house had to be a palace as seriously as did Thomas B. Croke. A French château and English manor house rolled into one, the structure had all the features of a castle—from the spired parapets and crocket-dotted roof to the immense fireplace in the baronial great hall. It was far too fancy a house for Croke, who was basically a farmer and agriculturalist, and before long he sold it to Senator Thomas Patterson, Democratic power and editor of the *Rocky Mountain News*. One morning while walking to work from the castle, at Eleventh and Pennsylvania, Patterson was attacked by rival Fred Bonfils, co-owner of the *Denver Post*, and a scandalous court suit resulted. Neither scandalous nor palatial today, the Croke "castle" is just another seedy old Denver mansion (*Denver Public Library Western Collection*).

At distinct odds with the castles surrounding it was the plantation house Governor James B. Grant built at Eighth and Pennsylvania for use as his governor's mansion. Designed in magnificent Southern colonial style, the thirty-room mansion had a billiard room, a bowling alley, and a combination ballroom and auditorium built especially for Governor Grant's inaugural ball. The house, whose grounds once spread over an entire block and even now sprawl from Pennsylvania to Pearl, was later purchased by mining and oil magnate A. E. Humphreys. It is one of the few Capitol Hill palaces still used as a private home.

even more ostentatiously Victorian than the city's houses. Built in hulking Gothic style or turreted Romanesque, they generally featured—often in the same building—every conceivable style of trim. They combined in one multiple-family dwelling as much design as their occupants would have lavished on half a dozen houses.

It is possible that the most pretentious home in Denver, fittingly the governor's mansion today, was the red-brick, colonial-style mansion at the corner of Eighth and Logan. Known first as the Cheesman residence and later as the Boettcher home, the estate stands guard like a lone sentinel, almost the last of the Capitol Hill mansions. Although the mansion is a mere four stories, far shorter than the skycraper office and apartment buildings around it, the latecomers are overshadowed by the home's stateliness and solidity. Built later than most of the Capitol Hill homes, by the Walter Cheesman family, the mansion was purchased in 1926 by Claude K. Boettcher, whose wife furnished it with a fortune in antiques—a $50,000 Gobelin tapestry purchased from the Russian government, a crystal chandelier that once hung in the White House, a French carved mahogany desk with copper trim and secret drawers. The house remained a private home until Mrs. Boettcher's death, when the state of Colorado reluctantly accepted it—although it was something of a white elephant because of its tremendous upkeep—and turned it into a governor's mansion. The year-round residence of the state's First Family, who live mostly in the upper floors, the mansion is open for public tours. (*Denver Public Library Western Collection. Photograph by Louis C. McClure.*)

Coming home late at night from an evening at the Tabor Grand Opera House, Judge and Mrs. Owen LeFevre would find the crouched figure of Baby Doe Tabor waiting for them in the doorway of their mansion east of Capitol Hill. The judge, Mrs. Tabor's lawyer, would lead the woman inside, listen to her woes, and dispense legal advice, for which he never charged. Mrs. Tabor was only one of the LeFevres' charities. From their mansion at Thirteenth and York, now housing Alcoholics Anonymous, Eva French LeFevre directed her many public causes, and few people in Denver could refuse her requests. Harry Tammen once declined to donate to the Children's Hospital fund, and his wife, remarking you couldn't turn down Mrs. LeFevre, gave the charity a fabulous pearl necklace her husband had recently purchased for her. When one of Denver's prominent madams died, Eva LeFevre followed the funeral procession in her carriage, saying later that this was her way of doing homage to someone who "always supported my charities." Long after the judge died, Mrs. LeFevre lived in the York Street mansion, furnished with pieces that once had belonged to Marie Antoinette, cared for by a few servants. As a concession to her age, she finally agreed to install a handrail at the side door of the house but refused to allow another in the middle of the front steps, telling her son-in-law, "I want my casket carried down those steps, and if I put up a rail, there won't be room." The steps remained unadorned, and when Eva French LeFevre died, a formidable woman in her late nineties, her casket was indeed carried down the expanse of steps at 1311 York Street.

Baron Walter von Richthofen was a Prussian nobleman who attempted to build a smart suburb on the prairieland east of Denver. The first—and for a time the only—house in "Montclair" was the baron's own, a crenelated castle-like structure which sheltered a carved head of Barbarossa and the von Richthofen coat of arms. The fortress' grounds also held a stable and milkhouse, connected to the house by a three-hundred-foot underground passageway; a moat supposedly inhabited by bears; a greenhouse; and a vast park. The baron lost his money in the silver crash, and the gray limestone house passed on to the Edwin B. Hendrie family, who spent $200,000 to enlarge the castle. Located in a quiet suburban area that eventually grew up around it, Richthofen Castle, 7012 East Twelfth Avenue, is still a private home (*Denver Public Library Western Collection*).

When bonanza king H. A. W. Tabor, Colorado lieutenant-governor and multimillionaire, moved his wife to Denver from their modest frame residence in Leadville, he bought a handsome red-brick villa at Seventeenth and Broadway. His austere wife Augusta balked at the twenty rooms and disapproved of the fancy furnishings and silver cuspidors that the servants would have to polish. She disliked the extravagance of it; Tabor had paid $40,000 for the house and another $20,000 to remodel it, but the Leadville cottage was more to her liking. When he led her to the steps of the front door, the reluctant Augusta told him, "Tabor, I will never go up those steps if you think I will ever have to go down them again." Augusta didn't, but Tabor did when he left her to marry divorcee Baby Doe in a Colorado scandal that cost him his political future (*Denver Public Library Western Collection*).

To make up for the snubs Denver society gave the second Mrs. Tabor, H. A. W. bought her a magnificent estate on Capitol Hill, 1260 Sherman, called "probably the finest residence in the State" when it was built in 1879 by J. W. Bailey. Baby Doe put a fountain in the living room and nude statues in the yard. Tabor put in the stable two lavish carriages— one black with white upholstery, pulled by two jet horses driven by Negroes in scarlet livery, and the other light blue to match Baby Doe's eyes. Although Denver society ignored the Tabors, national political figures and celebrities were less selective, and the Tabors entertained brilliantly. They continued to live in the lavish mansion even after Tabor lost his fortune, at which time—unable to pay their bills and with the utilities turned off—he hauled water from a well near the courthouse. The couple and their two children, who once had chased peacocks in the front yard, eventually moved from the Sherman Street mansion, now the site of an apartment house, to a tiny house and later to a simple room in the Windsor Hotel, where Tabor died. After his death, Baby Doe moved to her husband's once-productive Matchless mine in Leadville, where she lived in squalor until her death thirty years later. After her death many of the mementoes of her Sherman Street house were found tied in rags hidden in the mine shack.

When lusty Maggie Tobin—born in the Mississippi riverbed, bred in the rawest Colorado mining camp—became the immensely wealthy Mrs. J. J. Brown, she characteristically underwent no phenomenal cultural change, but she thought she did. Armed with millions of dollars and some outlandish clothes, she attempted to break into Denver society, which to a member snubbed her. As the late Lucius Beebe once remarked, Denver society itself had arrived just the week before, but Maggie, despite her homage and slavish courtship of the elite, was pointedly ignored. Even after emerging as the heroine of the Titanic disaster, the unsinkable Mrs. Brown, who was awarded the French Legion of Honor, was not recognized by the people who mattered. In an attempt to crash the portals of Denver's social arbiter Mrs. Crawford Hill, Maggie built her fantastic House of Lions at Thirteenth and Pennsylvania.

Inside, among the potted palms and gaudy hangings, Maggie entertained hordes of neighborhood children invited to consume quantities of lobster newburg and charlotte russe intended for Denver's elite, who never attended any of Maggie's parties (*Denver Public Library Western Collection*).

As Denver's 400 came and went, Maggie Brown stood as stoically as one of her stone lions at the gate of Mrs. Crawford Hill's Capitol Hill mansion. The building of the huge gray-brick mansion at East Tenth Avenue and Sherman was personally supervised by Mrs. Hill—whose blood was as blue as Maggie Brown's was red—and was designed for entertaining the capitalists, industrialists, public leaders, and socially prominent who minced through its marble halls and sat gingerly on the gold and ivory furniture. Guests were ushered through a magnificent reception hall, where they might watch Mrs. Hill make a timed entrance down the red-velveted stairs, lighted by a lamp from Thomas Jefferson's estate, to attend a ball in the palm room or tea or a cocktail party on the broad south porch. It made little difference to Maggie Brown that she would have found Mrs. Hill's soirees horribly dull compared with her own parties for visiting elks—royalty and theater people—who found her sphinx-headed lions and tapestried walls peculiarly charming and Maggie herself far more rousing than the formal Mrs. Crawford Hill (*Denver Public Library Western Collection*).

Like Maggie Brown, Lena Stoiber attempted to plow her way into Denver society, but where Maggie faltered at the gate, Lena, unaffectionately known to the Silverton miners as "Captain Jack," walked right in. Society, however, didn't curb Lena's eccentricities. Deciding that she didn't like her neighbor in Silverton, she had fenced her property line with a three-story wall. And when she had the same reaction to her Denver neighbor, she built a massive stone wall around "Stoiberhof." It was unfortunate that the wall protruded just far enough into the neighbor's yard to give him the right to demand that she take it down. But he wouldn't allow workmen access to his yard to demolish it. Lena said to hell with it and left the house, at Tenth and Humboldt, for an extended trip to Europe (*Denver Public Library Western Collection*).

Decorated with ferns, carved furniture, velvet draperies, and lavish
Oriental rugs, Stoiberhof beggared Maggie Brown's House of Lions
(*Denver Public Library Western Collection*).

It was fitting that when ex-bartender Harry Heye Tammen built his palatial Denver home (*second from right*), he did it with the same flamboyance with which he had once thrown twenty-dollar gold pieces at the ceiling of the Windsor Hotel bar, saying that the ones that stayed up there belonged to the management, the ones that fell were his. As co-owner of the *Denver Post*, Tammen was in palmier days when he built his mansion at 1061 Humboldt. The over-sized tile house featured an enormous inlaid wood staircase, designed and built by the Pullman Palace Car Company. The landing had a small balcony built to be used as a platform for Theodore Roosevelt when he spoke to a crowd of Tammen's friends. Marble fireplaces, Tiffany chandeliers, gold-leaf and carved mahogany ceilings, friezes with scenes from the *Rubáiyát of Omar Khayyám*, Florentine marble bathrooms, and carved cherubs' heads decorated the house. The living room ceiling was of intricately carved walnut, which Mrs. Tammen claimed made the room dark, and while the Tammens were away on a trip, a maid had it painted white as a surprise. The land on which the Tammen house stood originally belonged to Governor William E. Sweet, whose red-brick house (*right*) stood next door. Tammen's ponderous house seemed like a giant teddy bear ready to pounce on the houses of his neighbors, one of whom modified her house because of him. To the south of Tammen lived an old bachelor named Duncan and his spinster sister. To the lady's dismay the two men would stand on their separate porches swearing and yelling obscenities at each other, until finally, for decorum's sake, she built a soundproof room in her house, complete with fireplace and wall-to-wall carpeting, called the "cussing room," where they could swear—in private—to their hearts' content (*Denver Public Library Western Collection*).

Just as Tammen built a home that looked big and overstuffed like the affable Dutchman himself, his partner in the *Post*, Frenchman Frederick Bonfils, built a mansion as suave and as courtly as he was. The Bonfils home, a gracious, stately, pillared structure, stood at the corner of Tenth and Humboldt, half a block from the Tammen mansion. Less preposterous than Tammen's house, the Bonfils home had a long, flowing staircase that paused briefly at a window under the entrance portico. During a labor strike when Bonfils backed management, an armed guard was posted at the window with a machine gun.

71

The houses along the 1600 block of Washington, built about 1890, are a queer combination of every style of architecture available in the Victorian era—hulking gables, Grecian pillars, Italian windows, Gothic gargoyles,

Romanesque arches—along with a number of features thought up by the Victorians themselves: flashing stained glass windows and intricate cast-iron work.

The J. P. Kinneavy Terrace at Twenty-seventh and Stout was deemed so striking it was prominently featured in an 1889 issue of *Western Architect and Building News*. Built at a cost of $26,000, the building consisted of five units, each lighted by a court, and was so elegant it might have overcome the stigma of being an apartment building. Today the Kinneavy Terrace, whose name long has been forgotten, is painted white with blue trim and is almost unnoticeable (*Denver Public Library Western Collection*).

A conglomeration of styles, this building at Twentieth Avenue and Emerson has nearly every feature of Victorian architecture.

Typical of Victorian apartment buildings was this one at Thirty-second and Franklin, with its combination of delicate and hulking archways and gaudily decorated towers and roof line.

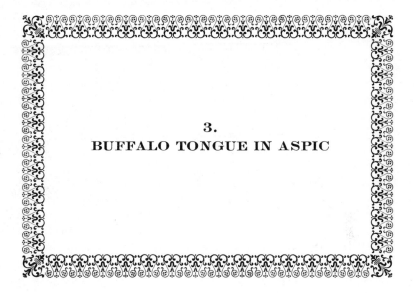

3.
BUFFALO TONGUE IN ASPIC

EASTERNERS WHO THOUGHT of Denver City as an outpost of savages were astonished to step out of their plush and polished Pullman cars into a splendid Victorian city. Used to the clapboard depots that dotted the Kansas prairie and Colorado flatlands, they marveled at the fine Union Station with its rambling stone and cast-iron building. Driving through Denver they were agog at the generously decorated houses and presumptuous buildings. But nothing astounded them as much as Denver's lavish hotels with their velvet carpets, their richly carved black-walnut furniture, the crystal-lit chandeliers and gilt mirrors, and the ornate bars and wine rooms. Denver's hotels were heralded from coast to coast—the early American House, where Grand Duke Alexis delighted female aspirants to society by stomping on their feet at a grand ball, and the Windsor, whose bar was home to Colorado's English royalty, political greats, and such colorful Westerners as Buffalo Bill Cody.

Erected in 1859 as the first fine-finished hotel in Denver City was the Broadwell House (*Denver Public Library Western Collection*).

Later generations lionized Henry C. Brown's Palace with its hallowed onyx halls; astute travelers still do.

The city's great tradition of hotels began with the Eldorado, the chinked-log cabin with log tower on top run by the Murats and Davide Smoke. The first year at the diggings was barely out when the settlement boasted a fine finished frame hotel to attract travelers, the Broadwell House, thrown up late in 1859 by J. M. Broadwell. When the hotel man had attempted to buy lumber for his enterprise from a Judge Wyatt, the judge had refused to sell, out of kindness, saying antelope would be grazing on the hotel site in less than three years, but Broadwell bought forty teams of oxen from disgruntled gold-seekers headed for home, put them to work hauling timber and lumber, and gathered the materials himself.

The Broadwell House opened formally in late 1859 with a fancy

"You that want a delicious bath at any hour of the day or night can be accommodated at Green's Star barbershop, in the Planter's House," announced the *Rocky Mountain News*, although it is doubtful that these unwashed people are lined up here for that purpose. Located on the southeast corner of Sixteenth and Blake, only a block from the Broadwell, the Planter's House was erected in 1860 to give the Broadwell competition (*Library, State Historical Society of Colorado*).

ball attended by the town's self-styled elite, dressed in "coarse but clean" linsey-woolsey and brocade, buckskin and broadcloth. A few months later the same swells paid a whopping ten dollars a plate to attend a smart banquet and speech that included an unexpected bit of drama. The evening's speaker, L. W. Bliss, acting territorial governor, was an antislavery man who made his views painfully clear to Dr. J. S. Stone, a Southerner in the audience. The

Confederate resented Bliss's remarks and said so, and Bliss threw a glass of wine in his face. Stone challenged the governor—shotguns at thirty paces—and two days later was gunned down in an infamous duel.

A two-story building later enlarged to three, the Broadwell contained an office, parlor, dining room, ordinary, reception rooms, over thirty bedrooms, and dormitories for employees. Damaged by fire in 1863, the hotel was forced to close, but it soon reopened as the Pacific House. General Sherman and his staff were entertained there when they visited Denver in 1866. Named the Broadwell again, the hotel, located at Sixteenth and Larimer, gave way in the late 1870's to the massive Tabor Block.

The name "Lindell" was supposed to remind travelers of the Lindell Hotel, an ornate St. Louis pleasure palace, and the word "West" in front of it was to distinguish the two—if, as the Denver management fervently hoped, someone confused them. Despite the effort, however, the Lindell namesake didn't quite measure up to the original, but it did rank favorably among the dreary structures that Denver City called hotels.

The original portion of the West Lindell was erected in 1860 as the branch store of a Santa Fe trader, but it was enlarged a year later and made into a hotel. Eventually the building boasted a bar, a billiard room, a barbershop, baths, a sample room, reception rooms, and bedrooms. A large porch with a hand-forged iron rail ran around the second floor, and for those who preferred to view Denver from dizzying heights, there was the third-floor glassed-in observatory with the first roof garden in the West. Located in a prime residential section at the corner of Eleventh and Larimer and guarded by stone lions, the West Lindell charged guests a stiff $1.50 to $2.00 a day.

Closed in 1878 for extensive remodeling, the hotel was reopened shortly afterward with an elaborate celebration at which John Pickle presided and G. W. King, the "greenback orator from Boulder" (whatever *that* was), gave a speech. An immense bonfire was built as a sideshow but soon got out of hand, and local firefighters had to be called; they quickly quenched the blaze—and

The West Lindell was a stylish place to go for Denver's *ton*. The more daring climbed to the roof garden and viewed Denver from a distance of three stories. Divested of any interest, historical or architectural, the West Lindell Hotel today is just one more of Denver's forgotten old buildings (*Denver Public Library Western Collection*).

their thirst as well. Soon afterward the Lindell began to decline. Its brick was stuccoed over and its three proud stories were reduced to two. Although the hotel still stands, it has been many years since a guest has confused the two Lindells—or indeed, remembered either one.

Not far from the West Lindell in old Auraria stood the Tremont Hotel, Thirteenth and Blake, noted in early history for its splendid receptions. Governor William Gilpin stayed in the Tremont in May, 1861, and was treated to a "fashionable" reception. Gilpin's successor, Governor Evans, fared even better a year later with a

81

"brilliant" reception. The host at both was M. Sargent, who did well not only by the notables but by all his guests. He let them sleep on Tucker's celebrated spring mattresses and fed them the Cherry Creek's finest offerings. Christmas dinner, 1862, was a veritable feast at the Tremont. It began with tomato soup, then went on to roast beef, pork, turkey with cranberry or oyster sauce, boiled corned beef and cabbage, beef tongue, and mutton, kidney, or antelope stew. There were three kinds of potatoes, seven relishes (including mangoes), and a dozen vegetables. Dessert was mince, blackberry, and peach pie, sago pudding, poundcake, charlotte russe, lemon, strawberry, and almond jelly, blancmange, nuts, and raisins, along with champagne, port, sherry, hock, catawba, and claret. It was no wonder that Christmas at the Tremont from earliest times was a Denver tradition.

Denver society was wild with anticipation when the American

House announced it would hold a lavish ball for the Russian Romanoff, Grand Duke Alexis, a twenty-two-year-old gangling giant with hands and feet as big as a Siberian peasant's, who had been buffalo hunting on the Platte with the great Pahaska. Accompanied by a brilliant entourage that included—besides Buffalo Bill—General Phil Sheridan, General George A. Custer, and Major George A. Forsyth, the royal Russian announced plans to attend the ball, to the delight of Denver's society matrons with eligible daughters who even then had latched onto the honorable American Victorian notion of title-buying. Thirteen rooms had been reserved and redecorated for Duke Alexis in the American House, and all of Denver hoped for invitations to the ball. Promptly at 9:30 on January 17, 1872, the anticipated night, Gillman's Band launched into the grand march, which was led by Alexis and Territorial Governor E. M. McCook's wife, who had ignored medical advice and risen from a sickbed to dance with the duke. To the sounds of brasses and drums the Russian and the governor's wife led the march until, as the final note sounded, Mrs. McCook slumped to the floor in a faint and had to be carried back to bed. She was a smashing success. The dance lasted long into the night as Alexis ogled the girls shamelessly, trod on their toes and their trains, and bumped into everyone. Denver society, whose manners weren't much better, was pleasurably outraged and talked about the grand duke for years.

Built in 1869 by cracker merchant John W. Smith, the American House, at the corner of Sixteenth and Blake, was severe and dignified, even plain, with rectangular windows and little style; but it was still Denver City's first pretentious hotel, and the Cherry Creek thought it very grand. The American House had no elevator but instead a graceful stairway with carved spindle bannisters and wine red treads. The hotel was furnished with silk-upholstered walnut couches and plush-bottom chairs. Beds were covered with feather mattresses, and each room had plush curtains, a bootjack, and a metal bathtub filled from pitchers of water carried by bellboys under the direction of Mr. Washington, the ceremonious Negro head porter.

The American House, Sixteenth and Blake, was the first of Colorado's Victorian hotels. Sparsely decorated on the outside, the hotel neverthe-less boasted an interior with all the delights of the nineteenth century—flowing staircase, walnut furniture, velvet carpets, and heavy draperies. The Blake Street addition was built sometime after the main portion of the hotel. Weakened by a Cherry Creek flood, both were torn down in 1933 and replaced by a gas station. To handle the overflow from the American House, the Inter-Ocean was built diagonally across the street. Far more luxurious than the first hotel, the annex, nevertheless, was less popular (*Denver Public Library Western Collection*).

From the day it opened in 1868, the American House was a brilliant success. The first register was replaced in a mere seventy-two days—it had 4,466 arrivals, an average of 62 a day. These included not only Romanoff royalty but such inveterate American travelers as U. S. Grant and Cyrus W. Field, who laid the Atlantic cable. Another hotel guest was Baby Doe, who had lived in the Windsor but had discreetly moved out when H. A. W. Tabor moved in. She left the American for the Windsor and notoriety when she married the bonanza king soon afterward.

At the height of the American House's popularity, its owner built the equally plush but never as popular Inter-Ocean Hotel across the street. Opened in 1873, the Inter-Ocean had a patent annunciator with wires to every room and a speaking tube on every floor. The lobby was fitted with a semicircular desk behind which hung a walnut key rack and card board. The reading room with its Brussels carpet and black walnut reading tables was heated by a grate set in a mantle of marbleized iron and lighted by a three-burner bronze chandelier. A dining room with three twelve-light chandeliers and heavy black walnut furniture, and a ladies' ordinary boasting a dove-colored carpet with light brown oak leaves and a Turkish border appealed to the Victorian traveler. The upper stories were sleeping rooms decorated with bronze chandeliers and a variety of window coverings in each room. Next to the window panes were folding inside shutters covered with costly lace curtains framed by satin lambrequins matching the room's upholstery and heavily trimmed with crimson heavy satin, and on top of all were rich velvet drapes trimmed with satin, yellow and black braid, and heavy bullion tassels.

Rocky Mountain News editor William N. Byers, who after a free meal generally spoke highly of his hosts in print, called the Inter-Ocean the "finest in the territory," but authoress Helen Hunt, who stayed in it a few months later, was less impressed and said, "It is one of the most depressing places I have ever seen." Apparently more of the hotel's guests sided with her than with Byers, for the Inter-Ocean never prospered. In 1874 it was purchased by Benjamin O. Cutter, who had made a fortune in the Caribou Mine

85

A stylish structure with a mansard roof trimmed with dormer windows, the stained-pink Inter-Ocean, stripped of its elegant furnishings, ended as a flophouse.

near Boulder and planned a $75,000 addition to the hotel. But he never carried out this plan, and in 1876 the hotel was auctioned off for $30,000. In the 1880's when the American House rooms were going for up to three dollars a night, the Inter-Ocean charged only fifty cents to a dollar—approximately what the rooms were renting for as flophouse quarters when the hotel closed a few years ago.

The Wentworth, left, was a smart uptown hotel, four stories of brick with balconies on two sides. The St. James addition had strong vertical lines, whereas the Wentworth looked horizontal, an incongruity that bothered neither proprietor nor guest. What was important was that the interior was elegant. To the right of the St. James addition was O. P. Baur's confectionary.

A guest is not allowed to do anything. There are waiters in every part of the house. I went in to supper. A waiter stepped up and pulled back the chair. I stepped to my place and he shoved the chair under me and when I got through he pulled the chair back. It was a little the best supper I ever ate . . . 17 kinds of bread 4 of potatoes 4 of eggs 8 of drinks and 37 kinds of meat. I had 3 kinds of bread one of eggs 5 of meats and chocolate.

This guest at the St. James in 1883 was noticeably impressed with the accommodations he found at this smart uptown hotel. In the letter he wrote home to mother he took a scant line or two to describe seeing Buffalo Bill and meeting relatives, but he devoted a page to describing the delights of the St. James—in his room were two marble-top bureaus with keys, two common chairs and a rocking chair, two gas lamps, a very fine mirror, and a telephone. The bathroom, which (he noted) was free of charge, had two faucets for every bowl, and it cost nothing to have his boots blacked.

Originally a frame building called the Wentworth, the early hotel was replaced by a brick structure with balconies on two sides and a balustrade on the roof, also called the Wentworth although Charles Wentworth, genial early proprietor, had long since moved on. In 1881 a splendid new addition was built, and to newspaper fanfare the hotel was opened as the St. James:

THE ST. JAMES
Completion of a Splendid New Edifice of Curtis Street
And the Opening of a Super Metropolitan Hotel
A Building That Stands a Splendid Monument to Enterprise and Sagacity
An Establishment that Will be the Pride of all People in Denver
Full Description of One of the Handsomest Hotels in the West
Points Personal and Otherwise in Praise of Two Worthy Citizens
Mr. A.H. Estes, the Pioneer Builder in Denver's New Era
Mr. David A. Gage, the Model Hotel Man of the East and West
A Reporter's ramble Through Their New House

All of these headlines were from the *Denver Tribune*, which aptly described the wonders of the "swell hotel of the town," including the cuisine, "which is beyond peradventure" and attracted many cattle-men and miners to "the principal hotel above Larimer." Although most guests were quite pleased with the dining room, the self-styled epicures of the Gout Club—which revolved around Judge Amos Steck, Ward Hill Lamon (who was putting finishing touches on his biography of Abraham Lincoln while staying at the St. James), and James B. Belford (the "Red-Headed Rooster of the Rockies")—preferred to sit on the iron-railed balcony and eat the meals John Elitch sent up from his nearby restaurant.

About the time the hotel began to decline, around the turn of the century, it was renamed the Regent, and a portion of it, as the first commercial all-movie house in Denver, put on what supposedly was the first nickelodeon show in the country in 1901. Much later the Fashion Bar originated on the ground floor. The entire hotel—the Wentworth and St. James addition—was torn down in 1960 to provide parking space.

The Alvord House was one of a number of smart Larimer Street hotels that flared briefly in popularity then dropped into anonymity. Built in 1875 as the Sargent House, the hotel was modern if not wildly elegant. It had two entrances (one for the ladies), a refrig-erated meat room where "meats can be preserved in perfect state for three weeks," a dining room with space for 150 adjoining a

88

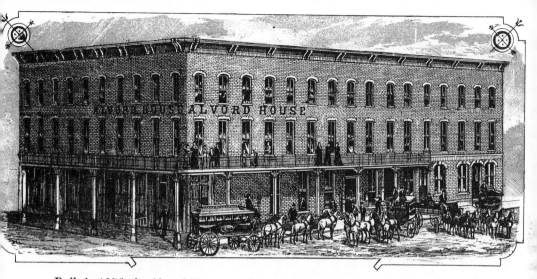

Built in 1875, the Alvord House was known as an excellent, if not extravagant, hotel in 1880 when this picture was drawn. Located at Eighteenth and Larimer, the hotel was soon overshadowed by the Windsor, built across the street.

"carving room," and a nurses' and children's parlor. Like the more extravagant hotels of the day, the Alvord catered to the Victorians' love of plumbing with Turkish and Russian, electric and common baths. Opened as one of the town's leading hotels, the Alvord "became the place to go above all when one wanted a delicious repast prepared by a master hand and wine of the ripest, richest flavor, iced to the 'nth' degree. Later they called it the Victor[y] and as such it dropped from the winnings."

Although the inside piazzalike court that rose in tiered triumph to the roof and the lace curtains tied back with heliotrope ribbons were designed to appeal to the ladies, there was little doubt that the Albany was a man's hotel. Buffalo Bill Cody made it his headquarters in later years. The Democratic decision to run William Jennings Bryan for President in 1908 was made in a traditional smoke-filled room of the Albany. Walter Juan Davis wrote his poem in the Albany bar, perhaps after deep reflection in his glass:

89

The Albany Hotel, designed after early Parisian buildings, was a charming complex of turrets, bartizans, and a hint of a mansard, with a bay window in every other room. (*Library, State Historical Society of Colorado. Photograph by William H. Jackson.*)

"When your feet hit hard and your head feels queer / And your thoughts foam up like froth on a beer . . . ." And among the Albany regulars who made their home in the saloon was Tom Marshall, the man who supposedly ran Bat Masterson out of Denver, who once asked the bartender for a pair of pliers, extracted his back tooth, and followed the operation with an admirable amount of straight bourbon.

Further evidence that the Albany was a man's hotel was its menu, noticeably devoid of confections and frivolities. The fare for New Year's, 1891, for instance, began with raw oysters with celery and consommé colbert then went to broiled kennebec salmon steak with sliced tomatoes and onion rings, sweetbreads, roast ribs of beef, wild turkey *farci* with game sauce, baked sweet potatoes, cauliflower au gratin, English plum pudding with hard or brandy sauce, cheese, and Java coffee. As a concession to the ladies, the menu also included boned turkey aux truffles, chicken mayonnaise, and charlotte russe.

The Albany was built in 1885 at a cost of $150,000 plus another $100,000 to furnish the 155 rooms and 50 private baths. The outside of the hotel, with its turrets and series of bay windows, was ostensibly French, but the inside was pure American Victoriana with a fountain in the lobby court featuring a marble Niobe.

Built by an Albany, New York, capitalist, the Albany was always a smart uptown hotel, catering to the town's businessmen when the cattle barons and mining magnates of its earlier years decreased in number. It was remodeled shortly after the turn of the century, possibly to appeal more to the ladies, with a number of stylish tea rooms—a concert room called "Bohemia," the Colonial Room where Signor DeVivo gave afternoon harp concerts, the Vineyard, the Orange Room decorated with tankards and ancient pottery, shields and electroliers, and the Peacock Room, where live birds strutted. A hotel annex was built in 1906, and another in 1912, but in 1937 the original Albany was torn down to be replaced by a one-million-dollar, seven-story building.

When General James W. Denver made his only visit to the city that had been named for him twenty-five years before, he stayed in the excellent, newly remodeled Markham Hotel. A few years earlier, when the building had been known as the Grand Central, a reception for President Ulysses S. Grant had been held there. Those occasions are the hotel's two claims to notability; the rest of its history has been commonplace.

Erected in 1872 at the corner of Seventeenth and Lawrence, the hotel was a plain, three-story building resembling the Alvord House. Ten years later, it was purchased by V. D. Markham, Thomas M. Patterson (later a senator), and Charles S. Thomas. The three men completely remodeled the interior and added a fourth floor with a mansard roof, Romanesque arches, dormer windows, a tower, and a collection of minarets to give the building class. They reopened it as an office block.

91

When it was known as the Grand Central, the Markham was a plain, unpretentious hotel (*Library, State Historical Society of Colorado*).

The Markham was a smartly remodeled hotel in 1882 when William H. Jackson walked uptown from his office on Larimer to photograph it. Originally a three-story hotel, it was given a fourth floor by its owners, who added nearly every trick of Victorian roof design to give it class (*Denver Public Library Western Collection*).

The newspapers gave far more editorial space to the opening of the Markham Block than to the opening of the Grand Central. "Everything throughout the hotel is new, clean and elegant, in fact there is not 5 cents worth of old appointments in the house," announced the *Rocky Mountain News*, which was to move its editorial offices and press rooms to the Markham a few years later. "The opening and reception last evening was a fine affair in every respect. Improper characters were carefully excluded, and the ball in the dining room was made an invitation affair, so that the company was a very pleasant one."

Despite the fact that the Markham was opened as an office block, it was quickly turned back into a hotel, lavishly fitted with black walnut and plush furniture and free bathrooms. Except for a brief stint as the *Rocky Mountain News*, it remained a hotel until fire gutted it not long ago.

When H. A. W. Tabor, whose life strangely paralleled Colorado hotel history, was living in poverty in a tiny Denver house, he received his mail at L'Imperiale Hotel. Every day Tabor would trudge to the respectable hostelry at Fourteenth and Court Place, which he listed as his address, to inquire of the indulgent desk clerk if there were messages for him. Eventually Tabor rallied enough to move to the Windsor Hotel, which he had helped maintain with his lavish living habits when both were younger and more flamboyant, and which like the almost destitute former millionaire was rapidly sliding downhill.

Never a lavish transient hostelry, L'Imperial was more of a high-class apartment hotel whose rooms were filled with families or honeymooners. Built in 1892 by E. J. Binford, a coal dealer, and called the Binford Hotel, the Tuscan Renaissance building was constructed of red rock and peach-blow brick with a red tile roof, at a cost of $65,000. Five stories high, the Binford had eighty-five sleeping rooms, each with a fireplace and a bath, plus a dining room in gold and white, a casino, and a roof garden. Plagued with financial troubles from the start, the hotel became an apartment building for bachelors in 1905 and by 1922 housed medical offices. In 1934 it was purchased by the Community Chest, later the United Fund, for $28,500 and torn down in 1963 by that organization, whose charity did not include preserving historic buildings.

Denver's worst hotel fire took place, oddly enough, in a notably unspectacular building—not in one of the city's flamboyant hos-

L'Imperiale Hotel (*Library, State Historical Society of Colorado. Photograph by William H. Jackson.*)

telries where the sparks of raucous doings might well have started a mighty conflagration, but in the unpretentious Gumry Hotel, 1725 Lawrence. The fire broke out one oppressive August night in 1895 when the twenty-year-old boiler room engineer, reeling from the late summer heat, stepped down the street for a beer. He was barely gone when the hotel boiler, drained of water, exploded, knocking out the back of the hotel and setting a tremendous fire. Twenty people were killed, including the owner, Peter Gumry, and

The debris of the Gumry Hotel after the 1895 boiler explosion (*Library, State Historical Society of Colorado*).

Charles Adams, the Indian agent who had negotiated the release of Mrs. Nathan Meeker and her daughter, held captive by Utes after the Meeker Massacre. Spectators came from all over the city to sort through the debris or merely to view the tragedy, and choice rooftop spots from which to watch the rescuers and scavengers rented for ten cents.

Nowhere did Colorado legend and Victorian elegance muster such a glittering display as in the immortal Windsor Hotel. Home to legions of Denver visitors ranging from Oscar Wilde to the great Pahaska, the Windsor with all its crystal and plush and black walnut was deserted long before they tore it down a decade ago, but its storied past lives on in countless volumes if not in as many memories.

The hotel was built in 1879 and intended as a pleasant middle-

The Windsor Hotel was the finest in the Rocky Mountains when it opened, and set a precedent in the West for years (*Denver Public Library Western Collection*).

class family hotel, but in the exuberance typical of the period, it was patterned after Windsor Castle and furnished with enough elegance to make a queen blush. (Fortunately for the Windsor, Colorado royalty had no such sensibilities.) There were three massive staircases (the "devil's head staircase" cast such a sinister shadow on the wall that H. A. W. Tabor was afraid to use it), seven miles of yard-wide Brussels, a gold-plated bathtub, and a tunnel under the street leading to Roman baths in the Barclay Building.

Colorado gold and silver gave the Windsor life, time and indiffer-

Everything was grand about the Windsor, from its lace antimacassars in the drawing room to the selection of frogs' legs right out of Washington Park Lake in the dining room. The rotunda could have housed a circus tent. Even the Windsor's suicides had style. They threw themselves off the heavily carved staircase and squashed on the marble below with barely a dent to the floor. The hotel held up remarkably even under such abuse (*Denver Public Library Western Collection*).

ence, decline; but the years in between, enough to make a man old, were filled with exquisite memories. Harry Heye Tammen, later co-owner of the *Denver Post*, was its bartender and in more prosperous years ahead was so fond of the Windsor that he wintered his circus troupe there, including the freaks. Buffalo Bill, the great, soused Pahaska, was limited to ten drinks a day, barely enough to wash down breakfast, but he solved the dilemma with the help of the Windsor barkeeper by taking his shots in beer glasses. H. A. W. Tabor hired bellhops to fill the tub for Baby Doe's bath at a silver dollar a bucket, despite the fact that the hotel had running water; legend says Oscar Wilde insisted that the wallpaper in his Windsor suite be changed with his moods.

The Windsor was envisioned by an English investment company as a simple brownstone, and when the firm realized that it had a Victorian palace on its hands, a mansarded five-story stone castle

Sports to the end, H. A. W. Tabor and Senator Ed Wolcott indulge in a twenty-year drunk. Artist Herndon Davis made it an enviable party by inviting a score of notables. Painted in the late 1930's, the portraits adorned the Windsor bar until the hotel was torn down in 1960 (*Duane Howell*).

with cast-iron porte-cocheres, it quickly sold out to three men who operated the hotel for a decade as the finest in the West. Not only famed travelers but Denver society lounged on the plush-bottom furniture and glimpsed itself in the diamond-dust mirrors. The Rho Zeta Club, an exclusive Denver bachelor group, for instance, gave several balls each winter on the specially built, resilient ballroom floor, and a girl who sat out a Rho Zeta dance risked her reputation.

After a heady fifteen years, the Windsor was on its way out, but the dying took two-thirds of a century. Denuded of its fine furni-

Viewed from the corner of Seventeenth and Broadway, the H. C. Brown Palace Hotel gives the unmistakable impression of a tug chugging into harbor (*Library, State Historical Society of Colorado*).

ture, covered with paint, and wallowing in grime, the Windsor was elegant until the minute they tore it down, and it will live on in splendor in a thousand legends.

When he couldn't sell the triangular cow pasture at the corner of his elegant Capitol Hill subdivision, Henry C. Brown built a hotel on it, and the H. C. Brown Palace was known, depending on the objectivity of the writer, as the finest hotel in the state, the finest in the country, or—hell!—the finest in the whole world.

Inside and out, "Palace" was an apt name for Henry Brown's hotel. It was nine stories high, built of Arizona sandstone in an Italian Renaissance style with animals and cherubs carved in the brownstone. Seven-and-a-half carloads (12,400 feet) of onyx lined the dining rooms, drawing room, cafe, bar, rotunda, and entrances. There were innumerable dining rooms and five bridal chambers, aptly decorated in "tints copied from a maiden's blush" and deemed "too beautiful and delicate for use," although, in fact, at a trifling $100 a day, there were a number of takers.

In the grand salon, delicately shaded silk furnishings reposed under an immense central medallion embedded in the ceiling in Watteau tints. "Here are blue clouds and soft fleecy clouds amid which rosy, blossom-wreathed cupids disport themselves," noted an opening promotion booklet. The main dining room, two stories high with a five-foot onyx wainscoting, was a confection of stucco-work pilasters and columns representing massive carvings of Japanese ivory.

The Brown, as it has been called lovingly for generations, opened in 1892 to host the Twenty-fifth Triennial Conclave of the Knights Templar, despite the fact that the building wasn't yet finished. The Knights dined regally in the immense parlors and drank elegantly in the banquet hall "christened with rich vintages mellowing for years in the cellars of aristocratic millionaires . . . brought hither in honor of that memorable week," but they were piled like peasants on cots in the halls since the bedrooms weren't completed.

Following the Knights through the onyxed halls was a procession of notables: Mary Garden, who turned the hotel upside down to

101

Basically a sensible brownstone on the outside (there is, of course, no sense of stinginess within), the Brown Palace does present occasional exterior delights, such as this cherub and his friends.

find a lost brooch, picked out of the gutter the next day by the doorman; Anna Held, who attempted to have the desk clerk fired when he refused to register her dog; William Jennings Bryan; Harry Lauder; Lillian Russell, who always stayed in a bridal suite; and Evelyn Walsh McLean, whose traveling companion was her Hope Diamond. In later days the Brown Palace was known as the summer White House when President Dwight D. Eisenhower vacationed in Denver.

Remodeled a number of times, enlarged by a towering addition across the street, the hotel, still replete with onyx walls and elegant dining rooms, has never gone downhill. Instead, time has added to

A handsomely illustrated grand opening promotion booklet pictures all phases of the Brown Palace—its rotunda with a fireplace so huge it later became a doorway, the grand banquet room, the grand salon, and a bathroom, an inestimable joy to the gimmick-minded Victorians (*Denver Public Library Western Collection*).

the dignity of Henry Brown's cow pasture. Mellow with a patina of years, the Brown Palace is still the finest hotel in Denver.

Barely had the Cherry Creek sourdoughs gulped down their first suppers of sowbelly and baking powder biscuits when they began craving the luxurious viands of their future wealth—fresh

The Brown Palace changed blissfully from a Victorian decor to one of heavy paneling and potted palms. It is to the Brown's credit that, although two men have been killed in its confines, no one has ever jumped the gilt rail that surrounds the nine-story rotunda (*Denver Public Library Western Collection*).

oysters and French pastries, frothy champagne punches and fine confections. It was beside the point that most of them never had tasted such edibles and many never would; their ravenous appetites and desire for unknown gourmet delicacies combined to produce strange gastronomic concoctions, bizarre combinations in the elegant Western restaurants soon to spring up—saddle of antelope, stuffed ptarmigan, venison à la mode, beaver-tail soup, and that most elegant gold-town treat, buffalo tongue in aspic.

Fresh seacoast oysters were produced in Denver that first Christmas—in jest if not in stew. Eastern newspapers carried heart-warming stories to the folks back home about the lavish holiday dinner their men were relishing on the banks of the Cherry Creek—oyster and oxtail soups, salmon trout, corned beef, elk tongue, venison, antelope, bear, mountain pig, pheasant, turkey, rabbit, duck, sage hen, prairie chicken, squirrel, prairie dog, snipe, mountain rat, white swan, quail, and sand-hill crane. Along with prickly pears and dried mountain plums the Cherry Creek men chose from a dozen kinds of wine and liquor. The Christmas feast account was written, however, by a notorious hoaxer, and while the men might have had their bellies full, it was not of oysters and oxtail soup but game meat and rot-gut—the Taos lightning that had arrived from New Mexico on Christmas Eve.

Before the next Christmas, however, Denver was well on her way to providing those very luxuries to anybody who could afford them. Prospectors who didn't know one fork from another, or even from a spoon, were seated on gilt chairs before velvet tablecloths, napkins at their necks, sloshing soup and guzzling wine from long-stemmed glasses, all under the benevolent gaze of crystal chandeliers and palm-rubbing hosts, who were happy to accept gold dust in lieu of mint coins.

Fred Charpiot, a Frenchman who arrived in 1860 at the diggings to peddle apples, opened the Cherry Creek's most lavish restaurant. Known from coast to coast for its elegant suppers and eccentric customers, Charpiot's played host to a legendary collection of big spenders—Rothschilds; Estes Park's Lord Dunraven; Buffalo Bill Cody; Ute Chief Ouray, who didn't add much class but plenty of local color; W. H. Vanderbilt, whose magnificent dinner at Charpiot's for his Western friends compared favorably with the munificent feasts he spread back East; and Grand Duke Alexis, whose plate of fish cost him thirty dollars.

Another Charpiot regular was Eugene Field, who involved Charpiot's in one of his most ingenious pranks. As a newspaper reporter, Field was well aware of the splendid reception Denver planned for Oscar Wilde, due to arrive fresh from Leadville triumph. The city stood in frank awe of him, not because of his erudition but because he had outdrunk a dozen miners at the bottom of a mine shaft. Denver's newly arrived society matrons, who just the day before had shed their mining-camp calicos for velvets and silks, were dressed in "sunflower" yellow and "lily" white—Wilde's favorite flowers—ready to discuss literature and aesthetics, whereas a week before they had talked about the price of salt pork and Arnholt coffee. Not to be outdone by their betters, the city's soiled doves were decorated in yellow sashes and garters and hair ribbons, chanting their own bit of literary artistry: "We know what makes the wildcat wild, but who makes Oscar?"

The story is told that Field, an inveterate practical joker, on hearing that Wilde's train was late decided that the *Tribune*'s managing editor would impersonate the lecturer and dressed his friend in a wig and fluffy collar. After taking the editor to Charpiot's and registering him as "O. Wilde," Field escorted the imposter about Denver, conspicuously pointing out buildings with his cane while the editor languidly contemplated his pastel gloves. When the real Wilde arrived, he was miffed at the lack of a reception committee, which had fawned all over Field's editor and gone home, and even when the committeemen realized the dupe and rushed back to the depot to apologize, Wilde failed to see any humor in the deception. Denver responded to the poet's lack of enthusiasm for the city's favorite prankster by an equally low opinion of his lecture on interior design.

The most elegant banquet ever held in Charpiot's—or in Denver, for that matter—was thrown by the English Lord Hague, a friend of Lord Dunraven's, who had just been acquitted of an Estes Park

106

murder. To celebrate his escape from the hangman, Lord Hague gave a plush supper party for a dozen friends at Charpiot's, and when he realized that with himself he had thirteen at table, he insisted that Charpiot send his niece to join them. After a lavish dinner accompanied by magnums of champagne, Lord Hague discovered that his guests one by one had slipped under the table, the young lady had retired, and he was drinking alone. Anxious for company, Lord Hague invited all the hack drivers in Denver to join him in a lengthy drinking bout that impressed Denver quite as much as Wilde's mine shaft triumph had impressed Leadville. For a week afterward mothers kept their children locked indoors out of the way of careening carriage drivers popping corks at each other in the streets. The feast, when its expenses were totaled a week later, had cost the host about $1,100 a plate for the original thirteen guests. Lord Hague thought it the finest party he had ever attended.

Although Charpiot's Restaurant was located in several different buildings, the most famous site was at Sixteenth and Larimer. One disgruntled diner said the restaurant building had no style, but most Denverites contended that it was merely "simple" (which was the same thing more kindly put). One even went so far as to call Charpiot's the most attractive building on Larimer when it was built in 1871, although it certainly wasn't that. Three stories of brick with a cast-iron front, the building sported polished French plate-glass windows and skylight, and vault lights covering the sidewalk. The basement boasted a parquet floor and walls with murals in oil. Across the front of the building in thirty-six-inch-high gilt letters was emblazoned "Delmonico of the West." The building cost $45,000. Charpiot himself ran the restaurant for several years, then turned it over to his relatives and went to France to live, where he died thirty years later full of raucous memories. The restaurant reached a pinnacle of popularity in the 1880's then slowly slid downhill. During World War I, Charpiot's was known as the California Hotel, and in the 1930's small businesses occupied its lower floors. The gilt letters long had been tarnished when in 1951 all occupants were ordered out of the once glamorous restaurant building; three years later it was torn down.

Fred Charpiot's Hotel and Restaurant originally occupied a third of this three-story brick and iron-front building at Sixteenth and Larimer. Later the restaurant took over the entire building. (*Denver Public Library Western Collection. Photograph by Duhem Brothers.*)

When Fred Charpiot's customers wanted a change of scene, they hied it over to Tortoni's, a restaurant at 1541 Arapahoe which was every bit as elegant as, if only slightly less extravagant than, the Larimer Street establishment. Opened in 1886 by John Elitch, who had made a tidy sum a few years earlier by strapping a sheet-iron stove onto his back and hiking to Durango to feed the prospec-

A dinner for this quartet cost a mere seven dollars in 1878. Grand Duke Alexis was charged thirty dollars for a trout supper. Banquets sometimes were one hundred dollars a plate (*Library, State Historical Society of Colorado*).

Tortoni's (*Denver Public Library Western Collection*).

tors, Tortoni's originally was called Elitch's Palace and catered to members of the Gout Club, athletes who admired the proprietor's physical prowess. In 1888, Elitch sold the restaurant in order to open an amusement park, and the new owners, who changed the name to Tortoni's, turned Elitch's place into an exclusive dining room. Furnished with a seven-tier solid mahogany china closet, an ornate bar that served one hundred, knee to knee, and a tiled floor where twenty-dollar gold pieces spelled "Tortoni's" the restaurant operated for thirty years but finally closed, a victim of prohibition.

A frequent Tortoni guest was Englishman Lord Ogilvy, who once overheard a farmer protest a charge of twenty-five cents for a baked potato.

"Didn't you enjoy it?" Ogilvy asked.

"No, I didn't," replied the outraged farmer. "Imagine charging twenty-five cents for a baked potato when that's what I get for a bushel of them."

"Well, my friend," the Englishman sympathized, "all I can say is that the farmer is on the wrong end of the potato."

Although a number of drugstores claim the honor, it generally is conceded that the ice-cream soda was invented as a fluke by Denver ice-cream vendor O. P. Baur. A caterer, baker, and confectioner, Baur came to Denver in 1876 to work at the City Bakery, next door to the nefarious Occidental Billiard Saloon. He attempted to open his own bakery and failed, then joined the Hayden Survey party in southern Colorado where, to the delight of the government, he arrested the problem of Indian pilfering by making great quantities of biscuits and distributing them to the roving Indians each morning. Returning to the Cherry Creek flush with triumph as an Indian arbiter, Baur opened a confectionary and became Denver's favorite caterer. Whereas respect came to Baur with a batch of biscuits and wealth with party treats, fame came with a glass of soda pop and a scoop of ice cream. Each morning a dyspeptic customer sat down in Baur's confectionary and ordered a glass of soda with ice. One day, when the customer arrived before the ice man, Baur persuaded him to cool the pop with ice cream. He did,

111

Baur's Restaurant, 1512 Curtis.

and the drink was so exceptional that Baur soon began offering it to other customers as the ice-cream soda.

The soda was Baur's most famous invention, but not his only one. He concocted French mints, crystal cuts, and Mija, an English toffee named for Theodore L. *Me*ier and John Joseph *Ja*cob, two employees who later became Baur presidents. While traveling in Mexico with his wife, the daughter of a Denver pickle maker, Baur discovered Aztec uses of cocoa and revived the ancient delicacy of chocolate-covered fruits and nuts.

Although Baur's didn't enter the restaurant business until 1891, it today operates dining rooms in two different Denver locations. Baur's old confectionary, replete with pink cherubs and marble counters, at 1512 Curtis, was gutted in 1970.

The Manhattan Restaurant (*Denver Public Library Western Collection*).

Larimer Street already had begun to decline in 1896 when Richard Pinhorn opened the Manhattan, a steak house at 1635 Larimer. "People come to me because I have what they want," replied the Englishman a few years later when asked why he wouldn't move to a more fashionable location. And he was right. Sometimes one thousand people a day crowded into the Manhattan Restaurant for twenty-five-cent dinners of charcoal-broiled steaks, french-fried onions, combination salads, and potatoes. Pinhorn once claimed that the Manhattan had served more charcoal-broiled steaks than any other restaurant in the world.

The Manhattan was a simple restaurant with plain china and linen, and Pinhorn was a formal man; nobody ever called him "Dick" more than once. He made a penny a meal profit when he first opened his restaurant and eventually grossed $750,000 in one year when his staff of waiters numbered sixty-five. Although popular, the Manhattan was a quiet place to eat, and Pinhorn's waiters were tough men to fight when they descended on a rowdy customer swinging salt shakers wrapped in napkins. They once stunned a noted boxer of the period who attempted a fight in the Manhattan and pushed him through the door before he knew what had happened.

Pinhorn died in 1922, leaving three-fourths of his estate to restaurant employees and the remaining quarter to a nephew in England. The employees ran the restaurant themselves until the nephew showed up, anxious to claim his fortune, and was put to work washing glasses. He returned to England. Without Pinhorn the Manhattan slid downhill and was only intermittently successful. It was sold and eventually closed, and in 1951 all the furnishings were sold at auction. Of all the items sold, knives brought a top price, two dollars a dozen, because of their fine condition, which buyers couldn't understand until an old-timer explained, "Back in the old days you didn't need a knife to cut one of Pinhorn's steaks."

What there was about oysters to appeal to the Cherry Creek settlers no one quite knew. They weren't very tasty after being packed in sawdust and ice and freighted across the prairie, but they were expensive, and they were high-class provender, and that was

114

Page from the Denver City Directory, 1880 (*Denver Public Library Western Collection*).

good enough for the *nouveaux* of Denver City. Nearly everybody in Colorado, whether or not he had tasted them or liked them, craved fresh oysters, and they were as much a part of Colorado legend as the bonanza kings who ate them. Louis Dupuy's Hotel de Paris in Georgetown was famous for its French cuisine but particularly for its oysters, which took much less dexterity to prepare than the less touted wild raspberry ice and *petits fours*. H. A. W. Tabor discovered Baby Doe and immortality as a rake when he slipped across the street from the Leadville Tabor Opera House one intermission for a snack of oysters and champagne at the Saddle Rock Cafe. It was only natural that a number of oyster houses would spring up in the most pretentious of all the Colorado cities, Denver.

Nearly all Denver restaurants served oysters, but several specialized in them. One was Mosconi's Fish and Oyster House, opened in 1879 on Blake Street by Louis Mosconi and still operated at 1645 Larimer by his son Dave sixty years later. Mosconi claimed he was the first restaurateur in the state to ship in fresh oysters, but oysters were common fare in Colorado long before Mosconi arrived. For a time Mosconi's restaurant was located across the street from the Tabor Grand in Denver, where during intermission, just like old times, H. A. W. and Baby Doe, now Mrs. Tabor, would stop in for an intermission oyster snack.

George Pell's tombstone.

Another prominent oyster house was Pell's, which like Mosconi's was located in a number of buildings. Opened in 1881 by George Pell on Arapahoe between Fifteenth and Sixteenth, Pell's Oyster House, later run by his son, wasn't closed until 1937. When Pell

117

died, an oyster-lover to the end, he was laid to rest under a rough granite slab carved with his name and a generous helping of oysters and fish.

4.
SCRATCH LANE

IF THERE HAD EVER BEEN any purity in Denver Victorian architecture—which is doubtful—it would have been found in the city's large office buildings. Although most architects never used less than two (and generally combined half a dozen) styles in public structures, the buildings were nevertheless simplified considerably in detail—no bargeboards or cupolas, and seldom in the earliest buildings cast-iron decorative trim, although the structures frequently sported cast-iron fronts. The Italian style was popular in the very earliest Denver buildings, where for a minimum amount of money—just enough to add several round-top windows and a few brackets under the cornice—a building might have a little class; but very quickly the builders became dissatisfied with simplicity, which was anathema to the Victorians, and cast-iron pillars and roof-top designs began to crop up along "Scratch Lane."

The tiny, two- or three-story shops, generally crowded between buildings just like them, showed the most imagination in decora-

"For the first time in our history we now have executive room of which we need not be ashamed," bragged the *Rocky Mountain News* in 1868, shortly after Lewis N. Tappan built his three-story building with the cumbersome stone arches. One of the territory's many capitols, the Tappan Building, which also housed the city's Masonic rooms, was the largest office structure in Denver when it was built. Next to it, on the southwest corner of Fifteenth and Market, was the Wells, Fargo Building, originally two stories, later raised to three to match the Tappan, then reduced to one (*Denver Public Library Western Collection*).

tive façades. They might sport any bit of whimsy, as a Victorian cottage did, whereas the larger office buildings and government structures were stuck with more conventional designs. As if to make up for their unimpressive size, the smaller buildings eventually combined the features of a dozen larger ones in their cramped

Millions of dollars in mail and gold shipments passed through this cigarette-advertisement-bedecked door back in the days when the building housed Wells, Fargo & Co.

Just down the street from Wells, Fargo, at 1444 Market, is this early brick building with Italian windows and a cast-iron front.

Nearly everything for the larder could be purchased from Birks Corn-forth, Pioneer Grocer, on Fifteenth Street between Blake and Wazee. Sacks of meal and self-rising flour, barrels of apples, potatoes, onions, fresh country produce, even patent medicines. The grocery, like Corn-forth, is long gone (*Denver Public Library Western Collection*).

façades. One might find three kinds of pillars, as many styles of windows, corbeling, cast-iron fronts, decorative doors, Romanesque arches, and stained glass, all in one two-story, twenty-five-foot store front.

The average Denver shop was two or three stories high, built of brick and decorated with heavy window detail and often a cast-iron front. Generally flat-roofed, the shop had fancy brackets under the cornice, which ended in upward flips. For the most part, these buildings are anonymous, cramped between others just like them. Often deserted, they aren't important enough to be noticed, let alone saved. 1728 Larimer.

1413 Lawrence (gone)

Undistinguishable from the parade of two-story, flat-top, slightly decorated buildings that lined downtown Denver, 1637 Larimer is notable
because it was the photographic studio of William H. Jackson during
the 1880's.

In more halcyon days
Jackson's studio was a
building worth seeing.

The larger office buildings stuck more doggedly to conventional designs. These buildings were foursquare structures with a kind of co-ordinated exterior decoration, marvels of fortuitous simplicity. Whereas their smaller cousins had to primp to keep up appearances, the larger buildings, firmly entrenched in purpose, acceptable for size alone like a grand dame who can be tacky because everyone already knows she is important, could afford to be plain.

(*text continues on page 161*)

127

Rodney Curtis and Clarence J. Clarke erected this once-jaunty brick building at 1634 Larimer in 1874. The lower story was finished with iron columns and plate-glass windows, the upper stories profusely trimmed with cut stone. The Curtis-Clarke Building once boasted twelve-foot-wide halls and a thirty-foot skylight, and every door was numbered with metallic figures. (*Denver Public Library Western Collection. Photograph by William H. Jackson.*)

Typical of the refinements of Victorian architecture was this doorway at Fifteenth and Market, now gone.

While upper Market Street dealt in human trade, lower Market, at Fifteenth, was another center of commerce. Here in this turn-of-the-century market one could buy nearly everything the farm produced. (*Denver Public Library Western Collection. Photograph by L. C. McClure.*)

The selection is less generous now.

One can still purchase some commodities in the Mapelli-Lindner-Sigman buildings along meathouse row.

When the extravagant H. A. W. Tabor decided to build the finest business block in Denver, he commissioned real estate dealer Colonel John Berkey to purchase the best corner in town. So Berkey approached John M. Eckhart, owner of the Broadwell House at Sixteenth and Larimer, who was at the moment napping in the basement of his hotel. Berkey asked the price of the lots, and Eckhart, half-asleep, told him $20,000. The real estate dealer, who had no paper, picked up a thin, curled shaving from the floor, wrote out an option, and woke Eckhart again to sign it. When Eckhart later protested the agreement, saying the amount of money was far less than the land value and insisting a signature on a carpenter's shaving was not valid, a judge replied, "It's as legal and binding as though written on twenty-four sheets of foolscap." Although Tabor paid a piker's price for the lots, he put up an extravagant structure. The stone for both building and sidewalk was cut to the architect's specifications near Cleveland, Ohio, and shipped to Denver at tremendous cost. Over the corner entrance, the architect erected a pediment with the symbols of the miners' trade and the words "Die Faustus," which someone had to translate for Tabor into "Lucky Day." The Tabor Block was one of the first of Tabor's holdings to go when the multimillionaire lost his fortune. Several years ago the proprietor of one of the shops in the building discovered scrawled on the basement wall, "I left this damn building on ——— thank God. H. A. W. Tabor." The date was obliterated. In 1898 the name of the building was changed to the Nassau Block, and in 1910 someone chiseled the name "Tabor" off the stone front.

Shortly after the Colorado Fifth General Assembly convened in the newly completed Barclay Block in 1884, it passed a resolution thanking the secretary of state for "selecting such comfortable quarters." Located at 1755 Larimer, the Barclay Block was five elegant stories of granite decorated with cast-iron columns and stained glass above every window. A tunnel in the basement connected with the Windsor Hotel to allow legislators to slip over to the Windsor bar without being seen from the outside—possibly the reason for the resolution. A collection of baths was located in the basement as well, where General Grant, Oscar Wilde, H. A. W. Tabor, and John L. Sullivan, along with lesser Colorado figures, whiled away the time, or legislators hid from office-seekers, who were at a distinct disadvantage when attempting to ask a favor from a sheeted figure sitting on a marble slab drinking ice water. After the adjournment of the Seventh General Assembly, the "Robber Seventh," the building management discovered that the legislators had taken with them everything they could carry out of their Barclay offices—diction-

One of the least chronicled of Denver's elegant old office blocks is the Cheesman Building at the southwest corner of Seventeenth and Larimer. Built in 1881, it was constructed of red brick with carved stone trim.

aries, cut-glass and bronze inkstands, spittoons, rugs, stationery, ink, chairs, and even desks. By 1950 the Barclay, long in the heart of Denver's Skid Row, was a favorite hideout of runaway girls, drunks, and destitute families. There were 250 occupants—142 of them children—roaming the rat-infested halls. In an exposé that shocked the city, the *Rocky Mountain News* described the filthy conditions of the Barclay with a series of articles calling the building "the shame of the city" and "a breeding spot for crime, disease and degeneracy."

The corner office once housed the plush ticket office of the Denver and Rio Grande Railway (*Denver Public Library Western Collection*).

Fifteenth and Larimer would always be the business center of Denver, Governor John Evans insisted when he built the massive granite Railroad Building there in 1888. But even then Denver financiers were heading toward Seventeenth Street, making the Railroad Building an anachronism only a few years after it was built. Evans' heirs let it go for the mortgage. Next to the Railroad Building, on the corner of Fifteenth and Larimer, stood the Pioneer Building, a smaller near-replica of the Railroad Building, built the same year. Both were torn down in 1971.

The massive redstone, granite, and pressed brick Colorado Mining Stock Exchange Building was built in 1891, served as mining exchange until the Colorado boom faded, and was torn down in the early 1960's. Seven

stories with a two-story tower, the structure was deemed "the most beautiful and costly temple of trade in the West" for its extravagant design, which included eight heads of Hercules, four gargoyles projecting from the corners of the square tower, and the heads of a bull and a bear in the semicircular archway at the main entrance. Inside, besides the stock exchange, was a large exhibition space for mineral display, a telegraph office, a gallery for visitors to observe trading, a mining library, and thirty offices. The miners of the day were so pleased with the building, and particularly its statue on top, that they started a movement to elect the architect to the Senate. He declined (*Denver Public Library Western Collection*).

139

For seventy years this twelve-foot miner with a lump of silver in one hand and a pick in the other looked out across Denver from the top of the Mining Exchange Building. It was incidental that he also served as a lightning rod (*Denver Public Library Western Collection*).

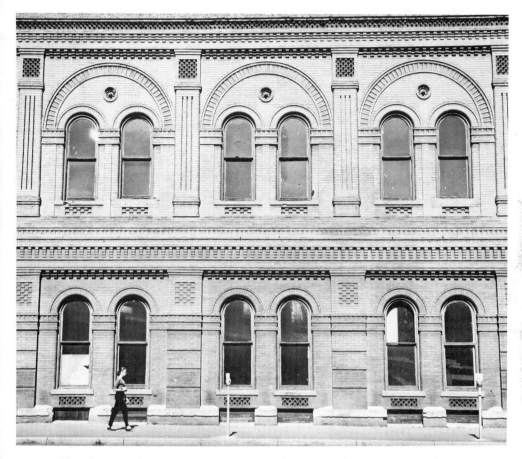

The days are long gone when passersby gawked at the Denver City Railway Company powerhouse, an orange-brick ornament at Eighteenth and Lawrence, with its bullnose corners, Romanesque arches, and heavy-handed detailing.

Con man Soapy Smith made his headquarters in the Chever Block during the affluent days after he gave up soap-hawking for organized bilk games. During Soapy's stay in the Chever Block, the Postal Telegraph Company was located on the first floor, and every Saturday night he would descend to the telegraph office, toss a silver dollar on the desk, and send a tender message to his mother, who never for a moment doubted that her son was one of Denver's upstanding citizens. After ending with "My heart's love to the dearest, sweetest mother that ever blessed a son," Soapy would return to his handsomely furnished office to direct the operations of his gang of sharpers. Built about 1880 by Charles G. Chever at the corner of Seventeenth and Larimer, the Chever Block originally housed the Exchange Bank in the corner.

The Iron Building, Seventeenth and Arapahoe, was an iron-foundry dream. Built of brick in 1891, the building, now gone, showed a front of solid glass and cast iron—pillars, fluted circles, Greek frets, brackets, and budding gable.

Denver Mayor Wolfe Londoner built this fanciful stone building at 1626 Arapahoe (which was torn down in 1969) as a palatial grocery store. A merchant who showed up in Denver in the early years, Londoner worked his way up from grocery boy to mayor with the unsolicited help of Denver newspaperman and prankster Eugene Field. During an early civic campaign Field concocted a story in which he wrote, "In appreciation of our colored citizens, of whom he is a great admirer, Wolfe Londoner invites every member of that race in Denver to come to his store at 4 o'clock this afternoon, where each will receive a present of a fine watermelon." While Field chuckled, Londoner searched Denver for enough watermelons to supply the crowd, but the effort was worth it. When the election results came in from the Negro district, Londoner had won by a landslide. Watermelons became a standard part of his campaigns and helped him win the mayoralty race in the 1880's. Not long after he took that office, however, election judges discovered that his workers had stuffed the ballot boxes, and a jury declared that, although Londoner was not personally involved, he was holding office by fraud. He appealed to the Colorado Supreme Court, which upheld the jury decision, and he was evicted only a month before his term ended.

"There is no building in the United States so universally quoted, or that is quoted with such uniform commendation as the Equitable, and to have been engaged in its erection has become among the building trades a veritable distinction," declared a plush, unequivocating booklet describing the delights of the recently opened Equitable Building, Seventeenth and Stout. In enviable prose the promotion publication described everything from the letter chutes to the men's rooms, going into ecstasies over the electrical wiring (to which it devoted three-and-a-half pages of description) and the radiator design.

Lavishly adorned with the "omnipresent" and "everlasting" E's, the interior of the Equitable was a Victorian palace. Above the serpentine staircase, the stained-glass window, featuring a naked little boy "quite unconscious of his bereavement," had been designed by Louis C. Tiffany's New York firm. In the lobby was a collection of admirable talents—mosaic vaulted ceilings, splendid swinging doors ("singularly solid and serviceable. The superiority of the swing is uncontestable."), and intricate dull bronze electroliers "shaped like round medieval bucklers, from which issue convoluted stems, which have a laughable resemblance to French horns, but Denverites like them."

Colo. Ex. Jour. Oct 1889   THE BOSTON BLOCK, DENVER.   FRANK REISTLE, ENG. DENVER. Denver — Building!

When Bishop John Spalding refused $60,000 for Wolfe Hall, a girls' school, he was chastised by the Episcopal Board of Trustees. A year later he sold the land at Seventeenth and Champa for $120,000 to the builders of the Boston Building. Erected in 1889 the Boston Building was nine Italian Renaissance stories, constructed of red sandstone quarried at Manitou Springs (*Denver Public Library Western Collection*).

147

The façade is rusticated masonry—the stone laid with receded mortar—decorated with five carvings in Byzantine low relief.

There were few tears when the city tore down the decrepit and deserted granite City Hall in the late 1940's. Viewing Denver from a triangular plot, now a parking lot, at Fourteenth and Larimer, the old City Hall, despite its neglected state in later years, had helped make Denver history. It was nearly destroyed in 1894 when Governor Davis H. ("Bloody Bridles") Waite called out the Chaffee Light Artillery and commanded it to train its Napoleons and Gatling guns on the stone walls while he ordered the police and fire commissioners to resign their offices, alleging that they had refused to stop Denver gambling. The two stayed in their offices, and the governor recalled the troops after three days, but the officials eventually were removed by court order. Denver's madams filed into City Hall to pay their "protection money," and through those same doors marched many of Denver's aldermen, one of them the city favorite, Martin Currigan. When the councilmen were considering purchasing Mullen ditch, part of Currigan's district, he exploded. "Pay money for that little ditch," he yelled. "Hell, no. I can spit half-way across it."

"You're out of order," admonished the council president.

"I know I am, Your Honor," Currigan replied. "If I weren't, I could spit clear across."

(*Denver Public Library Western Collection*.)

"One of the conspicuously inconvenient, ill-arranged, cramped, dark, and inadequate public structures evolved by 'bureau architecture,' . . . wholly unfitted for present requirements," wrote the usually mild historian Jerome C. Smiley about Denver's Federal Building. Begun in 1884, completed eight years later, razed in 1965, the structure, commonly called the old Customs House, stood at Sixteenth and Arapahoe. The U.S. government paid H. A. W. Tabor $65,000 for the site and considerably more—$570,500.52, in fact—to build the gray sandstone, steam-heated, dome-topped edifice. The massive building, considered ugly when it was built and uglier as it grew progressively soot covered and slummy, was beheaded of its tower in the late 1950's, and with a noticeable lack of protests from history buffs, was torn down in 1965. (*Denver Public Library Western Collection. Photograph by L. C. McClure.*)

Daniels, Fisher & Co. is as intricately entwined with Denver history as any building in the city. Early society matrons shopped in its elegant clothing departments before every prominent Denver social event. So did the prostitutes. The store's proprietors knew the madams were good for the girls' expenses, so they let them charge to their heart's delight, then billed the madams—adding a hefty mark-up for propriety's sake. When Oscar Wilde visited Denver in 1882, D&F advertised that he would attend the store's fifteen-dollar-suit sale. He didn't, but a number of Denverites did in hopes that they would catch a glimpse of him. A frequent patron was Baby Doe Tabor, who sent her coachman for a clerk to show her merchandise in her carriage. The store originally was known as W. B. Daniels & Company, then Daniels, Eckart & Company, and eventually, in this building at Fifteenth and Larimer, Daniels, Fisher & Co., commonly called D&F or "Fisher's." An early store buyer, in his enthusiasm at getting a good wholesale price, once ordered several hundred gross of trouser buttons—more buttons, Daniels remarked wrathfully, than there were people in the state. But the enterprising employee approached several keno parlors in the city and sold the buttons for counters at a profit (*Denver Public Library Western Collection*).

In 1875, Daniels & Fisher moved to Sixteenth and Lawrence and began what with many changes and additions would become a Denver landmark for eighty-five years. This façade was on Lawrence Street.

The Venetian bell tower that has loomed over Denver for half a century was copied after the Campanile of St. Mark's Square in Venice and completed in 1911. Part of a plush addition to the original building across the alley, the tower was designed in Italian Renaissance style by F. J. Sterner.

For years the store's symbol, the tower represented Denver to many of the city's residents. Election results were flashed from it, school classes and even a wedding were held in the upper floors, and nearly everybody in Denver at one time or another paid twelve cents to view the city from the high lookout.

It wasn't until Denver's banks became more affluent, with more money to protect, that they became staunch, fortresslike edifices. The early bank structures were no less fanciful than the buildings surrounding them. Denver's first bank was in a flimsy shack at Fourteenth and Larimer, the first mint being in a pretty brick building that looked as much like a shop as a coin factory. Located at Sixteenth and Market, Clark, Gruber & Co., Denver's mint, was opened in 1860 to coin "mint drops." During the Civil War, Clark, Gruber money was more valuable than Federal greenbacks not backed by gold reserve. After the war the government, not sure if Clark, Gruber could mint U.S. money legally, purchased the building and used it as a gold-buying office (*Library, Historical Society of Colorado*).

155

Clark, Gruber's banking affairs were taken over by Jerome B. Chaffee's First National Bank, Fifteenth and Blake, which opened in 1865 with capital of $200,000 and a building worth almost a quarter of that. The First National, the first Colorado bank to receive a charter under the national banking laws, didn't prosper until 1880 when its cashier, David Moffat, took over as president. The bank eventually moved from its Blake Street corner to an uptown location (*Denver Public Library Western Collection*).

Reminder of earlier banking
days is this First National
Bank clock, salvaged from a
previous bank building and
mounted behind the First
National, Seventeenth and
Welton, erected in 1958.

A gentleman might wait for the stage, discuss his business affairs, or just count his money in the handsome C. A. Cook & Company Banking House, as pictured in *Harper's Weekly*. Located at Fifteenth and Blake, the building was luxurious for 1860, with a floor, a fine counter, and Gothic-framed pictures tilting down at the customers (*Denver Public Library Western Collection*).

Harper's Weekly was either inaccurate or unconcerned about time lapses. This drawing of C. A. Cook & Co. was printed in 1866, a year after the company had ceased to exist. The First National Bank is across the street; Walter Cheesman's drugstore, where the Colorado National was located, is across the street from the First National to the left in the picture (*Denver Public Library Western Collection*).

Opened in a corner of Cheesman's drugstore, the Colorado National Bank of Denver was founded by the city's prominent Kountze family. The brothers Kountze hauled an eighteen-hundred pound safe across the prairie by oxcart, a thirty-five-day trip, for the smart bank building they would erect on early "Scratch Lane," Fifteenth and Blake. Across from the First National, the Kountze Brothers Bank opened in 1864; two years later it became the Colorado National. In 1882, the bank was shuttled to Seventeenth and Larimer. Thirty years later it moved to its current location, Seventeenth and Champa.

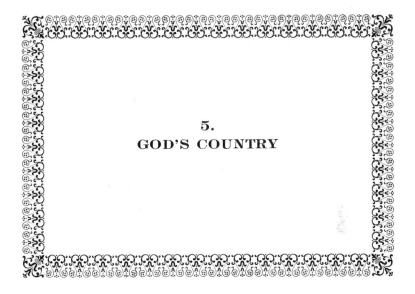

5.
GOD'S COUNTRY

DENVER CITY nearly beat itself to death patting itself on the back for its religious tolerance. Nearly every early newspaper account of Denver's churches lauded their hand-in-hand ways of working together, their respect for one another, their liberal attitudes. Congregations flocked in and out of each other's church buildings with the same agility that their staunchest members had jumped one another's mining claims a few years before. They even contributed to each other's building funds. In another city, a Methodist preacher and a Roman Catholic priest might have been antagonists, but in Denver the fiery Colonel John M. Chivington and the gentle Bishop Joseph P. Machebeuf were keenly aware that they worked on the same side of the Lord. When Father Machebeuf asked Colonel Chivington for money to build a Catholic church, the Methodist replied, "But I am just about building a church of my own."

"Very well, you are about to begin," replied the priest, "but I have already begun; my case is the most urgent." And Chivington handed over a generous sum.

Denver's first preacher was a Cherokee Indian, John Beck, who accompanied the Russells, Denver's first settlers, to the Cherry Creek in 1858. More interested in gold than Golgotha, Beck did no preaching, and the first church service was not held until the following fall when a Methodist lay preacher, George Fisher, officiated to the shuffling of cards in one end of the temporary chapel. Although the number of churches in early Denver was disarmingly small, especially when compared with the number of saloons, the religious fervor of the congregations was high, and Denver City was a great attraction to early preachers who saw the sins of the world flourishing in the raw town. The Bible carriers flocked to Denver with the love of God and man shining in their faces and a rifle tucked under the buckboard. They were no fools, these early men of God, and it is to their credit and that of their austere wives (whom history records with considerably less kindness than it does the prostitutes) that Denver became a city at all.

Their services were held in saloons, generally the only buildings large enough to hold a congregation, and the gamblers and drinkers, if they didn't stop playing and imbibing completely, at least toned down the noise of their chips and glasses in deference to the men of God. The preachers were a variegated lot, bound together by their zeal in carrying the Gospel. The Methodists sent the fierce John M. Chivington, who was later a colonel in the Colorado Volunteers—the hero of the Battle of Glorieta Pass and the villain of the Sand Creek Massacre. Bishop Jean Baptiste Lamy of Santa Fe, New Mexico, dispensed the kindly but zealous Father Machebeuf, the much-loved Father Joseph Vaillant of Willa Cather's *Death Comes for the Archbishop*. Another of the early Bible pounders was Parson Tom Uzzell, a hell-raiser with the heart of a saint and the fist of a miner. He once told an unwilling congregation he cornered in a saloon, "The man or woman who will get a miner drunk and take his money is the lowest skunk in Christendom. I shall be mighty glad to officiate at the funeral of such a sinner any minute."

162

Denver's first church, fittingly, was Methodist, for the Methodists were
the most zealous of Colorado's early Christians. The church was organized by the Reverend William H. Goode and the Reverend Jacob Adriance
on August 2, 1859, as the Denver City Mission. Later, under the name
of the Lawrence Street Methodist Church, the congregation erected an
inspirational cathedral at the corner of Fourteenth and Lawrence shortly
after the Cherry Creek flood (*Denver Public Library Western Collection*).

163

Fewer than twenty years later, the Lawrence Street Church, too small for its burgeoning congregation, was sold to the Salvation Army. While waiting for their grand new church to be completed, the Methodists held services in the opera house. (*Denver Public Library Western Collection. Photograph by George L. Bean.*)

There was much work to be done by these men of God, no tea drinking in the parlor or officiating at covered-dish suppers; there was the work of the Lord—tending the sick, aiding the poor, comforting the weary, traveling from camp to camp to carry the Gospel. The hard-working Father John Dyer, the self-named "Snowshoe Itinerant," unable to support himself by the collection plate, became a mail carrier in the rugged Hoosier Pass country, traveling on skis between parishes to deliver the mail and attend to his congre-

Trinity Methodist Church rose in medieval Gothic splendor at the corner of Eighteenth and Broadway in 1887. Built at a cost of $200,000, the church had an organ costing $30,000, more than the entire cost of the Lawrence Street Church (*Denver Public Library Western Collection*).

gation, the living and the dying. There was plenty for a preacher to do with the dead, too, for the death rate was high, increased by

(text continues on page 170)

Long hemmed in by the city that grew up around it, Trinity still sends its spire 182 feet into the air, but it is nearly unnoticed among the nearby buildings towering above it. Despite the commercial neighborhood, Trinity is still one of Denver's grand cathedrals.

When he platted his addition to Denver, Governor Evans told a specu-
lator named Witter that he would build a Sunday school in the Evans
section if Witter would erect one in his. The governor carried out his part
of the bargain (nobody remembers whether Witter did) and built this
chapel as a memorial to his daughter Josephine. Completed in 1878,
the chapel was deeded to the Methodist church by Governor Evans debt
free with the stipulation that the property never be made liable for any
debts and that it always be associated with religious teaching or worship.
In 1889 a larger building, Grace Community Methodist Church, was
built to adjoin the chapel and was used for worship by the congregation
until 1953. For the next few years Assembly of God members met in the
old Methodist Church, and in 1958 the site was purchased by the University of Denver for a parking lot. During the 1930's, Grace Church had
been used as headquarters for Depression charity—from handing out
bread to dispensing shaves and haircuts. In a laudable effort to save the
historic Denver building, the University of Denver, instead of tearing
down the chapel, decided to move it to the University Park Campus.
Assisted by a gift from the Evans family, which had been connected with
the school from its inception, DU had the building dismantled stone by
stone and reassembled, from sandstone foundation to cast-iron cresting,
in a parklike setting on the University campus.

Built in 1883 this building at Twenty-fifth and California was originally the First German Methodist Episcopal Church. Like many small neighborhood churches that grew up in Denver, it is weathered and unkept, but nevertheless dignified by age and years of service.

168

When the Episcopalian faithful began casting about for a site for their church, they spied the already consecrated spot recently deserted by the Methodists, a modest church at Fourteenth and Arapahoe; so they purchased the tiny frame building in 1862, built an addition in front, and named it St. John's Church in the Wilderness, for Denver was as wild to the Episcopalians of the 1860's as the deserts of the Holy Land had been to the Christians eighteen hundred years earlier. Before they purchased the church, Episcopalians had held services on the second floor of a saloon, and it was to their credit that they were able to persuade the management to suspend the lucrative Sunday morning traffic for the church hour (*Denver Public Library Western Collection*).

The Romanesque cathedral of St. John's in the Wilderness, no longer in heathen confines but in the midst of a splendid Victorian city, was built in 1880 and destroyed by fire in 1903. The present St. John's Cathedral at Fourteenth and Clarkson was completed in 1911 (*Denver Public Library Western Collection*).

epidemics, poor living conditions, and violence. Of the first twelve burials from an early Denver church, two of the men had been executed for murder, five had been shot, one had committed suicide, one had died in delirium tremens, and only two had expired of natural causes.

(text continues on page 179)

Emanuel Church, built by the Episcopalians in 1876, is located on the site of Denver's first Sunday school. The oldest existing church structure in the city, Emanuel was a Jewish synagogue in later years.

"... and, My Dear," wrote General Larimer to his wife, November 22, 1858, "when you see Rev. Plezes, tell him that we have reserved four lots on the corner of Arapahoe and Seventeenth streets for the first Presbyterian church. This of course, is conditioned upon the building of a church within one year." As a man of God, the general was sorry the church didn't take him up on his offer, but as Denver's founder and principal landholder, he couldn't have been too disappointed at having to keep his valuable lots. The first Presbyterian service by an ordained minister was not held until August, 1860, when fifty of the faithful met in a schoolhouse for worship, made plans to rent a house, appointed a sexton, and allowed the minister $10 for board. The congregation's new church was not built until 1864. Located on Fifteenth Street between Lawrence and Arapahoe, the brick church, thirty-seven by sixty-five feet, cost only $6,000. Despite a split in its congregation, however, Central Presbyterian Church, as the little chapel was called, grew so quickly that by 1876, the congregation had erected a $50,000 Gothic cathedral. The church, which was slated to cost $32,000, was so expensive that the members couldn't afford a roof, so an enterprising trustee solicited money from Denver's saloonkeepers, who handed over enough for a substantial slate roof. Possibly in an off-handed tribute, the roof was designed with eight diamonds on one side and seven on the other, and became known as the "Church of the Seven Spot of Diamonds."

173

In 1888 the Central Presbyterians purchased eight lots at Seventeenth and Sherman, erected a $22,000 parsonage, and laid the cornerstone for a new Romanesque church. The old one, at Eighteenth and Champa, was carted off to a new location and eventually burned. Its remaining stones formed the foundation of Montview Boulevard Presbyterian Church. Completed in 1892, the new Central Church cost $165,000.

174

No group of religious buildings more aptly fit the Denver *Republican*'s 1890 round-up of churches description of "stately piles of brick and stone" than did the city's Roman Catholic edifices. From humble beginnings in frame houses and log cabins, the Catholic churches soon began sending sandstone spires toward the heavens. Although their houses might yet be simple and the luxuries of life far in the future, Denver's Catholics were anxious that their places of worship in the Kansas Territory wilderness should be glorifications of the Lord. Father Machebeuf and the Reverend John B. Raverdy arrived in Denver City in 1860, found a congregation of two hundred Catholics waiting for them, and began organizing the city's first Catholic church. Discovering that the foundation of the church building at Fifteenth and Stout had been abandoned because of debt, Father Machebeuf raised money to complete the structure. Christmas Mass, 1860, was held in the newly finished St. Mary's. (*Denver Public Library Western Collection. Photograph by William G. Chamberlain.*)

Despite the growth of Catholic membership in Denver during Bishop
Machebeuf's thirty years of service, from one small chapel to a diocese
of forty-nine churches, the old St. Mary's, refurbished from time to time
(shown here after spire and side aisles were added), continued as
Denver's Catholic cathedral long after the bishop's death. Land for a new
cathedral, Immaculate Conception, was purchased in 1900, but the
church itself was not completed until 1921 (*Denver Public Library Western Collection*).

Whereas Denver's Protestant churches usually were designed with one imposing steeple, the Catholic churches were symmetrically styled with twin towers in front. Typical of the early Catholic churches, although built well into the twentieth century, is St. Cajetan's Ninth and Lawrence.

It rather surprised Denver that the first thing the city's Jews organized was a cemetery association, but in the prevailing atmosphere of religious tolerance, they didn't say a word about it. For the most part the Protestants were relieved, however, when the Jewish contingent of the city eventually built a proper church. Temple Emanuel was organized in 1873, and two years later the first temple was erected. A second temple was built sometime later at the corner of Twenty-fourth and Curtis, and in the late 1890's this synagogue at Sixteenth and Pearl was completed. One of the few Moorish buildings in the city, Temple Emanuel differed radically from the prescribed Denver church style with its Far Eastern towers and interlacing geometrical designs (*Denver Public Library Western Collection*).

Built to glorify God, Denver's early schools took no chances on offending with ill-designed campuses but were happy to please Him in every style of Victorian architecture. Gothic, Romanesque, Tudor, Italianate, and Mountain Jigsaw—any of the styles popular in houses and office buildings were likely to be found in Denver's school architecture, if not all in one building, at least within the confines of a single campus. Unlike some of Colorado's colleges with their continuous architectural design, the campuses of the Denver schools were either a pleasing polyglot of styles or school-boy grotesques, depending on the viewer.

Typical of this conglomeration of styles was the University of Denver, which had an architectural direction that changed with every wind. Few other areas of Denver encompass such a pre-ponderance of styles in so few acres. At the entrance to the campus is a Romanesque fortress, down a hill a California-mission-style church. A few yards away stands a brick fort and behind it a library in Andrew-Carnegie-learned. Just as incongruous, although built later, are Tudor and Italianate buildings with a sprinkling of postwar modern, and only recently was the University rid of its so-called temporary buildings, wooden barracks culled twenty years before from Amache, a Japanese relocation camp in south-east Colorado.

The University of Denver, originally a Methodist seminary, still bears overtones of Methodism, although it is no longer officially church-connected. It was begun in 1864 by that erstwhile Christian, Governor John Evans. Opened as Colorado Seminary, the school eventually was located in a smart brick schoolhouse across the street from Evans' home. Despite the governor's paternalism, the seminary failed and closed its doors for a thirteen-year hiatus. Reopened in 1880 the fledgling school, renamed the University of Denver, soon plunged into a series of financial crises. At best, the school enlarged the Arapahoe Street building that grasped it in Romanesque clutches, and made plans for a campus on the out-skirts of town; at low ebb, the University's chancellors fought a tense battle to keep the little school's head above water.

Because land was donated (by a reformed drunk) and conse-

179

University Park was a treeless prairie when University Hall was erected in 1890. Across from "Old Main," right, is Iliff School, a theological seminary built by the family of cattleman John Wesley Iliff. Loretto Heights College lurks in the background.

quently free, the University decided to locate its campus on a thirteen-acre site just south of Denver and in 1890 built a Romanesque bastion to hold its entire arts and sciences operation. Titled "University Hall," the structure was known, as these first buildings are, traditionally if not affectionately, as "Old Main." A group of University faithful boarded the special excursion trains from downtown Denver to the campus to witness an inspired, if hot and dusty, groundbreaking; and several visitors succumbed to the land promoters hawking homesites in the nearby prairie residential area ambitiously known as University Park. Most of the school's

Shown under construction is Buchtel Memorial Chapel.

professors, who were supposed to lend a scholarly aura to the neighborhood and set the pace by purchasing the first lots, could ill afford the homesites since the school was notoriously in arrears in paying their salaries; and when it did reimburse them, it often was with land in that very neighborhood.

The school's financial floundering eventually leveled off under the twenty-year chancellorship of Henry Augustus Buchtel, who took over the University in 1899 when its indebtedness was nearly $200,000 and rumors were circulating that Old Main would be turned into a glue factory. Despite looming foreclosure, Buchtel

181

Chamberlain Observatory reared its bald pate in 1894 just a few blocks from Old Main. Dean of the arts and sciences college Herbert A. Howe personally journeyed to New York to purchase lenses for the observatory's telescope, and on the return trip, since there was no adequate place to store them, he placed them in his Pullman berth and slept in a chair so that they might ride in safety—another example of the sacrifices man has made in the service of the Almighty (*University of Denver*).

not only pulled the school out of its financial quandary but managed to garner the money to erect several University buildings. The chancellor, whose brother was married to P. T. Barnum's

Looking like any small-town library and probably built on the plans of one is Carnegie Hall, erected shortly after the turn of the century and paid for by a donation from Andrew Carnegie (*University of Denver*).

daughter, had an ability to raise money that was legendary, and the school trustees who worked with him chuckled over the story of a little boy who had got a coin lodged in his throat. After several attempts to extract it, his mother finally said in desperation, "Send for Chancellor Buchtel; if anybody can get money out of him, he can."

Among the buildings for which Buchtel was responsible was the brick, fortlike Science Hall, its corners stretched upward in a stockade design, today a student terror. Nearby in Carnegian splendor is the old library, partly financed by the steel magnate himself. A Greek revival shell decorated with the horrors of dying Victoriana, Carnegie Hall was student union to generations of collegians, some of whom heard William Jennings Bryan speak in

183

its halls. Not far away from Carnegie (DU building sites were not platted but seemingly sprinkled about the prairie like sagebrush) rose the mission-style Methodist church, Buchtel Memorial Chapel, an architectural fancy so blatantly out of place with the other campus styles that the architect refused to have his name connected with the building. The idea for the chapel came from Buchtel's wife, recently returned from California, who decided the church soon to rise on the campus should resemble a coastal mission.

In later years the school switched to Tudor-style architecture, then to a stark brick-look, chosen because it was inexpensive. Today, with the irreverence typical of students for the only slightly old, DU's collegians dread classes in the school's older buildings and devoutly hope that Old Main will again have a chance to become a glue factory.

It was a quick glance but a good hour's drive straight across the open prairie from the University of Denver to Loretto Heights Academy. Separated by faiths but bound together by a zealousness to educate Colorado's young men and women, the Methodist preachers and the good sisters of Loretto paralleled each other in building schools of higher learning in Colorado.

The first sisters of Loretto, Joanna, Ignatia, and Beatrice, followed Bishop Machebeuf to Colorado in 1864 and opened a school in a frame house at Fourteenth and California, eventually St. Mary's Academy. Twenty-five years later the sisters dedicated a Catholic college for women on Mount Loretto, southwest of Denver, and built a handsome redstone structure alone on the prairie "where our girls who are to be wives, and kindly rulers and preservers of homes, can learn something of the grand mystery of silence and modest reserve," approved the *Colorado Catholic* when the building was completed in 1891. "The feminine readers . . . will pardon the writer, when he tells them that their sex should be infinitely more lovable if more silent."

Early one morning in November, 1891, the sisters and their fifty-one students boarded the Circle train in downtown Denver, rode to the stop nearest their newly completed school, and hiked

184

Heat and lights had not yet been turned on when the sisters of Loretto and their students moved into Loretto Heights Academy. Built in Romanesque style, a tower in the center flanked by two pitch-roof wings, the building has a heroic-sized statue of the Virgin Mary above an entrance arch bearing the inscription "Fides, Mores, Cultura."

the final two miles to find upon arrival in early evening that heat, lights, and water had not yet been turned on. To their further frustration, bedding and food, loaded onto wagons that morning at St. Mary's, had not yet arrived. It was after nine, and even the Mother Superior was in tears, when the burros finally plodded up the hill, and the women ate a cold dinner and went off to bed in an unheated building. That was only the beginning of Loretto's trouble.

The school was a mere three years old when the sisters faced financial ruin. As Chancellor Buchtel would do a few years later, Mother Praxedes Carty decided to forestall impending mortgage foreclosure by pleading in person with the insurance firm holding the mortgage.

"Sister, get your veil and shawl and come with me," she said impulsively to a nun she met in the hallway of the school. The sister obeyed, and the two were on their way to Denver before she asked where they were going.

"To Milwaukee," answered Mother Praxedes, explaining that was where the insurance company holding the note was located.

"But Mother," said the sister, "I have scarcely more than a handkerchief with me."

"It's the same with me," replied Mother Praxedes, "but we'll make out some way." And of course they did. Just as Denver businessmen have learned since, it was impossible to argue with an impassioned Lorettine defending her school. The two women arrived at the office of the insurance firm at the moment its officials were voting on the foreclosure. Mother Praxedes not only saved the fledgling school but enabled it to go on to become an important Colorado college. Originally the entire school, the main hall, today Loretto Heights College's administration building, now divides its original functions of classroom, dormitory, study room, dining hall, infirmary, and student activities center among a complex of twenty-five buildings.

Like Loretto Heights College that was to grow up several miles to the
south, the entire Regis College was quartered in a single building, "Main
Hall," built in 1888. As administrative office, living quarters for both
students and Jesuit priests, classrooms, chapel, and dining hall, the
building was a grand structure in size and stature, a Greek revival-style
building with columns and a Greek pediment. Unlike many campus
"old mains," whose innards have been turned into offices for underling
professors or mailrooms or freshman classrooms, Main Hall is still an
important part of the Regis campus that grew up around it. Until
recently it contained the college's seismograph station, and it still houses
two chapels (*Denver Public Library Western Collection*).

187

Denver was not ten years old when the Episcopal church decided it was time to build a church-oriented girls' school. The Methodists and Catholics already had begun teaching the faithful; for the Episcopalians, time was lagging. Named Wolfe Hall for the Eastern millionaire who put up most of the money to finance it, the Episcopal school was located at Seventeenth and Champa, the present site of the Boston Building. Erected in 1867, the building was a smart red-brick Gothic structure with a combination gable-mansard roof.

In 1888 the girls left the Champa Street school and moved to Fourteenth and Clarkson into a handsome building that included, among other things, an art studio. Each Wolfe Hall student was required to furnish six table napkins, six toilet towels, three pillowcases, three sheets, one pair of blankets, one counterpane, tablespoon, dessert spoon, teaspoon, dinner knife and fork, napkin ring, umbrella, waterproof cloak and overshoes, Bible and prayer books, and one rug. An early guidebook admonished, "no eatables, except fruit, may be received from home." Wolfe Hall was torn down in 1920 and replaced by Morey Junior High School (*Denver Public Library Western Collection*).

There was no nonsense about separation of church and state in Denver's
early public schools, for what were the city's good citizens paying taxes
for if not to instill the fear of God in their boys and girls? And as the
parochial schools held no monopoly on religion, they also had none on
architectural fantasy. The school board sanctioned no paring down of
style to save expense. It might economize on books or teachers' salaries,
but to cut down on the architectural trivia of the schoolhouse was un-
thinkable parsimony. Victorian school architecture is exemplified by the
Corona Street School, smack in the heart of Quality Hill at Eighth and
Corona. Built in 1890 at a cost of $70,000, the school, later called Dora
Moore for one of its principals, was lavished with sandstone and terra
cotta trim, stained glass, carved arches, indented brick, and corbeling.
Even the chimney that peaked in the center of a square formed by four
massive corner towers sported a few immodest designs on its sides.

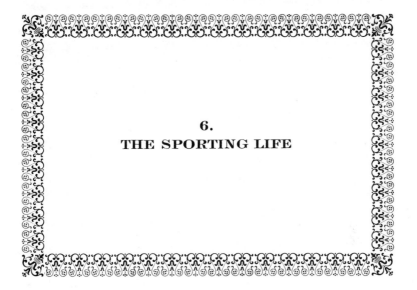

6.
THE SPORTING LIFE

THE FIRST SOUNDS of welcome to fall upon the ears of the gold-seekers arriving in Denver were the come-ons of the fleecers, the enticements of the gamblers—more aptly called bilks—who promised gold without the drudgery of scooping it out of the Cherry Creek. Barely had the pioneers knelt to thank the Lord for safe deliverance from the tribulations of the trail when they were off to the godless dens of the montebanks, where they generally lost what money they had left from the journey to stake their prospecting. In early 1860, by modest count, every fifth building in Denver City and Auraria was a saloon, every tenth a gambling hall, and those in between not always reputable. The total of gaming houses and bars was just under thirty, twice that of hotels or restaurants, and so much higher than that of churches that the righteous were shamed.

The gambling halls and saloons, usually the same thing, lacked even a semblance of luxury, having dirt floors sprinkled with water to keep down the dust, canvas walls, poor ventilation and lighting, and plenty of cheap whisky. Many offered free liquor to gambling customers, and nearly all guaranteed a free funeral for a paying patron killed on the premises.

None of the earliest saloons was more iniquitous than the Denver House, although it was only slightly worse than the average Denver gambling hall. This establishment was a long, low, one-story building with log walls and a ceiling hung with white sheeting. The room was usually crowded with filthy, swarthy men who consumed enormous quantities of cigars and liquor, generally purchased at outrageous prices. The games were rough—and high; a Denver visitor early in the city's history noted that he saw the county probate judge lose thirty Denver lots there in less than half an hour one Sunday morning and later observed the county sheriff pawning his gun for twenty dollars to spend at faro.

Three-card monte was the game that appealed to the uninitiated (since they thought the odds obviously favored the player), and to the dealer (since he knew he was nearly unbeatable); a good one might net $100 a day. Standing behind his little table, the dealer would select three cards from the deck, show their faces to the crowd, and begin his pitch:

"Here you are, gentlemen; this ace of hearts is the winning card. Watch it closely. Follow it with your eye as I shuffle. Here it is, and now here, now here, and now" (laying the three on the table with faces down), "where? If you point it out the first time you win; but if you miss you lose. Here it is you see" (turning it up); "now watch it again" (shuffling). "This ace of hearts gentlemen is the winning card. I take no bets from paupers, cripples or orphan children. The ace of hearts. It is my regular trade, gentlemen—to move my hands quicker than your eyes. I always have two chances to your one."

To stimulate the action, if it seemed slow, a plant in the crowd around the table would throw down a twenty-dollar gold piece and point to the winning card, and the dealer would scowl and pay up. Encouraged by this obvious piece of good luck, some newly arrived dupe would plunk down his money only to find that the dealer's

Patronized by a swarthy crowd of bearded, unkempt men, such as those pictured above playing monte, in this illustration from *Harper's Weekly*, the Denver House was open twenty-four hours a day for those who wanted to buck the tiger (*Denver Public Library Western Collection*).

hand was indeed faster than the player's eye. When the action slacked off, another one of the dealer's friends would slyly win a bet to pump up dwindling interest.

The dealer-plant gambit was a popular one in Denver for fleecing strangers, and nobody played it to perfection as did Jefferson Smith. Standing on a street corner with a box of soap bars, "Soapy" Smith would wrap several of the bars in ten-, twenty-, even fifty-dollar bills, then casually throw them into the pile, all the while imploring his listeners to take a chance on selecting a bill-wrapped bar for a mere five dollars. Generally the customers were slow in taking the bait until a friend stepped up, threw down his money, and gleefully unfolded a "shinplaster" from inside the soap wrapper. The crowd would rush in, anxious to take advantage of the hapless vender, blissfully unaware that the money he had seemingly wrapped around the soap had instead been slipped into a slit in the box. When interest fell off, another of Soapy's accomplices would pull out a bill-wrapped bar, and the crowd would surge forward again. Soapy's victims, of course, had one advantage over the prospectors swindled by the three-card-monte boys at the Denver House: they ended up with soap.

By virtue of the fact that even gamblers couldn't operate twenty-four hours a day, the Denver House provided beds as well as bilking tables and called itself a hotel. After one look at the Denver House accommodations, Horace Greeley dubbed the hotel the "Astor House of the Gold Fields" and noted that its prices were no higher than those of a luxury hotel back East—except for liquor, twenty-five cents a drink for "dubious whiskey, colored and nicknamed to suit the taste of the customers." One night in the Denver House was enough for Greeley, who probably didn't mind sleeping on a grass mattress in one of the six sheet-shrouded cubicles or filling his wash basin from the barrel in the corridor (customers were expected to dump the dirty water on the floor to help the management keep down the dust) as much as he minded the constant uproar of the gamblers just a canvas sheet or two away from his room. After only a few hours the *Tribune*'s august publisher slipped over to Count Henri Murat's Eldorado Hotel, although not

194

The harpist and balloon seller posing happily for the photographer in 1875 might have dodged bullets fifteen years earlier had they blocked the entrance to Charley Harrison's place. Known as the Criterion Saloon and later the Mozart Billiard Hall, the building was the hangout of the notorious killer Charley Harrison, whom Bat Masterson called the best gun-handler in the West. The Railroad Building, torn down in 1971, later stood on the site—Fifteenth and Larimer. (*Denver Public Library Western Collection. Photograph by Duhem Brothers.*)

before the patrons of the Denver House had prevailed on him to give a speech. Highly inspired by what he'd seen and heard that night, Greeley gave a strong address attacking gambling and drinking, which was "received with good humor" by his listeners, who respectfully put down their cards and glasses until he had finished.

The Denver House was notorious under that name, although it is better remembered by the picturesque "Elephant Corral," probably an allusion to its size. Robert Teats changed the name of the gambling hall when he purchased it in the early sixties and transformed it into a complete caravanserai with a large corral for horses and wagons protected by armed guards hired by the house. Teats had no interest in gambling and collected no percentage of the winnings, but merely rented his tables to dealers, although he felt the ire of an occasional hapless dupe who lost his stake in Teats's establishment. The hours were the same in the Elephant Corral as they had been in the Denver House: play went on night and day to the screeching of a makeshift orchestra ensconced behind a sheet-iron enclosure thoughtfully provided by the management. In case of a shooting, the musicians could drop to the floor with no more damage to themselves than a hole in the fiddle, which was no detriment to the kind of music they played.

Eventually the Elephant Corral burned down, although its name lingered on as one of the most intriguing in Denver history. Inspired by the interest the name produced, artists sometimes included an anachronistic "Elephant Corral" sign or building in pictures of a much later Denver.

Almost as notorious as the Denver House, although its reputation was inspired by the owner rather than just general iniquity, was the Criterion Saloon, which was less imposing than its competitor.

Charley Harrison was a slick-tongued Southerner, a gunslinger as full of Dixie chivalry as of Western meanness. He showed up in Denver in 1860 on the run from a Mormon posse and quickly set himself up at the Criterion as the head of Denver's multitudinous wicked element. He had fourteen notches on his gun when he arrived and promptly added a few more, one to note the death of a

Despite the fact that the Elephant Corral, earlier known as the Denver House, burned to the ground in 1863, it remained a picturesque subject for painters. In this 1867 view of Denver, painted by A. E. Matthews, the Elephant Corral is pictured in full glory, four years after the first Elephant Corral was demolished. To the right of the Elephant Corral sign was the famous Palace Theatre, and the building on the corner next to G. W. Kassler & Co. housed the popular Occidental Billiard Hall (*Denver Public Library Western Collection*).

Negro who insulted his white Southern sensibility by calling him by his first name.

Ed Jump had built the Criterion, an unimpressive two-story frame building with a false front, and advertised a table to rival Delmonico's along with a Denver novelty—a wine cellar. Charley bought into the Criterion and established it as his headquarters. The clientele was such a lawless bunch it prompted the townsfolk to call a meeting in Mr. Graham's drugstore and organize a vigi-

In 1932, although boldly advertising horses for sale, this spot calling itself the Elephant Corral probably was a junk yard (*Denver Public Library Western Collection*).

lante group. Charley's men easily infiltrated the organization, which responded by forming an inner group of ten, called "the Stranglers," to handle the burgeoning lawlessness. The pranks of Harrison and his boys eventually fired the wrath of the sedate William N. Byers, who attacked the gang in the *Rocky Mountain News*. A few of Charley's cohorts spirited Byers over to the Criterion one morning bent on foul play, but Charley just as quickly sneaked him out the back door and escorted him to his newspaper

A newcomer to the Colorado gold fields looks warily at a card game while supporting a friend, far gone in his cups, who might be susceptible to the wily dealers. To the right, a luckless player, befittingly barefoot, bets his last coin on number five, while behind him a befuddled argonaut, who probably questioned a deal, leaves the game at gunpoint. A stabbing in the background attracts no more attention than do the two moribund musicians playing on top of the bar (*from* Frank Leslie's Illustrated Newspaper, *January 9, 1864*; *Library, State Historical Society of Colorado*).

office. The scare was enough for Byers, however, who thereafter tempered his attacks considerably.

After an ill-fated attempt to ally Denver City with the Southern cause in the Civil War, Charley went to war on the side of the Secessionists, and he never came back to the Cherry Creek. The

Chase and Heatley opened Denver's first elegant gambling hall, the Progressive Club, in 1864 at the suggestion of several prominent Denver businessmen who wanted a high-class "recreation games club" where they could be relatively certain of getting a good drink and a fair deal. The mountain man in the foreground might well disapprove of this 1866 *Harper's Weekly* sketch of the Progressive, since both chandelier and floorboards are out of place. Gas wasn't piped into Denver buildings until 1870, and the Progressive was built directly on the ground without benefit of flooring (*Denver Public Library Western Collection*).

Criterion later became the Mozart Billiard Hall, run by little Count Murat, who was as unsuccessful in the saloon business as he was in most of his ventures.

Since the Occidental Billiard Hall, located in the Fillmore Block, was open twenty-four hours a day, it is doubtful that the reading room advertised on the sign was much of an attraction (*Denver Public Library Western Collection*).

"Between thieving and gambling, the former is far more honorable than the latter," declared the *Rocky Mountain News* in its never-ending campaign against the gambling dens. Periodically successful, Denver's finer element didn't really succeed in ridding the city of its gambling dens until sometime after the turn of the century. Three-card monte was outlawed early in the camp's life, but the city legalized it again in 1860, causing one member, the righteous G. W. Clayton, to resign in indignation.

For the most part, with only occasional shutdowns by the forces of morality, the gambling saloons ran wide open. In 1865 the dens, located for the most part on Denver's main business streets, enticed their customers from blocks away with brass bands and stringed orchestras. A customer might saunter in for a dance with a partner of just about any nationality, then step up to the bar for a two-bit slug of whisky, plunk down another quarter for a cigar, and wander to either side of the room to spend the rest of his capital on any game known to the profession. Although the Elephant Corral and the Criterion were immensely popular, they were short-lived and soon were dimmed by the dazzling lights of such elegant variety halls as the Corn Exchange, the Cricket, and the Progressive.

The Progressive Club was opened by Denver's most spectacular gambling operator, "Big Ed" Chase, on the advice of several prominent businessmen who wanted a smart "recreation games club." Born in Saratoga, New York, and brought up in the hotel business, Chase reportedly opened the Progressive with $1,500 won at poker while working as a railroad brakeman, but chances are he had local backing, for the Progressive was no piker. It boasted Denver's first billiard table, hauled across the plains by oxcart, along with an abundance of other gaming tables and bars. Upstairs were private rooms for games run without a limit, and a customer could drop as high as $200 on double cards, $100 on singles. Chase watched over it all with his steely blue eyes as he sat on a high stool with a sawed-off shotgun lying conciliatingly across his knees. Something of a paradox among gamblers, Chase mixed easily with Denver's upper crust; the Methodist minister and later infamous "butcher" of the Sand Creek Massacre, Colonel John M. Chivington, along with the Third Colorado Cavalry staff in full regimentals, attended the saloon's opening in 1864 and publicly asked the Lord's grace on the gambling hall.

The next of Chase's many gambling ventures in Colorado was the Cricket, located on Blake not far from the Progressive. Opened in 1870 by Chase and his brother John, the Cricket had everything to assure the success of a variety hall—a freak show with a three-headed body, loud music, gambling tables, and ten-cent drinks. It also hosted several balls—one advertisement noted that proceeds were to be given to the poor, "P.S. We're the poor"—but none as notorious as the gathering of the "frail sisterhood" at the first grand ball of Denver's demimonde, in 1874. The *Denver Tribune* reported the event in full color, calling it a "hilarious and eventful occasion:"

The Cricket was ablaze last night. Mr. Charley Ward organized a ball in special honor of the nymphs du pave.

From shortly after dark till far into the morning, bevies of the frail sisterhood were making the Cricket their objective point. In fact, it was after 1 o'clock this morning when the festivities fairly commenced.

An initiative "drink all around" furnished the necessary stimulus for a start and, from that hour till long after sunrise, there was a continuous dance—waltz, schottische, polka or quadrille,—the intermission being occupied by fortifying the "inner man," or woman.

There were blondes and brunettes, and every other conceivable style of beauty that is manufactured to order.

Among the most conspicuous were Belle Derring, Sadie Bent, Eva Hamilton, Elva Seymour, Kittie Wells, Laura Winner, "Gertis," "Cora," "Jennie Logan," "Emma Marsh," "Dutch Nellie," "Mormon Ann," "Frankie," "Annie."

The absence of Zell Glenmore, Mesdames Preston, Williams, French, Perry and Rhoda, was noted and much commented upon.

Many "new-comers" weakened sensibly about 4 o'clock A.M., just when the " '59ers" were beginning to enjoy themselves. And it was broad day before the last of the revellers left (or were cricket) from the ever-notorious Cricket.

Thus ended the first grand ball of the demi-monde.

The Cricket was only one of a multitude of variety show houses that decorated Blake and Market Streets with lights and blazing signs. Under the guise of warning its readers of the addresses to avoid, a Denver newspaper printed a list of variety halls with directions for finding them. Starting at the American House, at the corner of Sixteenth and Blake, the article led the reader along the north side of Blake to the Corn Exchange where "on the pavement a glaring bulletin announces 'Wit and Mirth,' and the 'Queen of Song,' and 'a Free Concert.' This invitation leads to an extensive 'Bar,' back of which are all kinds of gambling devices, and questionable entertainments, kept up throughout all hours of the night and day." Another of the gambling saloons connected with the ubiquitous Ed Chase, the Corn Exchange was a less prosperous enterprise than the Progressive. Nevertheless, it did capture the attention of the public when the *Rocky Mountain News* ran a gleeful little

Tenants of the Fillmore Block were interested in all kinds of entertainment. Here, just around the corner from the Occidental, the combination of a stuffed bear and a photographer draws a crowd. (*Library, State Historical Society of Colorado. Photograph by W. G. Chamberlain.*)

tidbit about Ed Chase's wife. Dressed in men's clothes, Mrs. Chase had rushed into the Corn Exchange and attempted to shoot Nellie Belmont, "a waiter girl in that free and easy resort . . . who is alleged to have been too intimate with her husband for some time past." The next year the still indignant Mrs. Chase divorced her husband on grounds of adultery, charging he had kept Nellie in a cozy little love nest at one of his clubs. If Nellie had more permanent designs on Chase, she was miffed when the saloonkeeper

Once one of the most obstreperous corners of Denver, Fifteenth and Blake, site of the Occidental, is now a occupied by a sedate gas station. The bleak building next door was originally the City Bakery.

married another woman in 1877, then took a third wife in 1880.

Assuming his reader had succeeded in going past, the reporter continued his descriptions of Denver's principal haunts: "A few steps further Westward brings us to the 'Occidental Hall' . . . . Going up a single flight of stairs we enter a large Hall blazing with light and flashy ornamentation . . . . Placards of 'beer 10 cents' appear among the gas lights, and numerous 'Beer Girls' promenade the hall as waiters. About the walls are hung bulletin boards in flaming colors with the following advertisement: 'More talent, Miss "So and So," the great Prima Donna and soprano vocalist.' "

While the reporter continued on, describing the Progressive and the Cricket, the reader generally got no farther than the Occidental at the corner of Fifteenth and Blake. Located in the Fillmore Block, built on the site of the Cherokee House where the 1863 fire had begun, the Occidental itself featured shows hot enough to start another conflagration. Up the single flight of stairs, a member of Denver's sporting fraternity would find not only Miss So and So performing in the fancy hall but a commodious bar and tables featuring a dozen games of chance. Despite the fact that Fillmore had built his business block with double brick fireproof walls and a double floor lined with concrete in order to protect the more sedate businesses sharing the building from the twenty-four-hour-a-day clamor of the Occidental, Colorado state legislators meeting in a room next to the gambling hall reported that they wrote bills to the slapping of poker cards and made up reports to the rattle of roulette wheels.

Not always the scene of naughty entertainment, the Occidental hosted an 1872 concert by opera singer Stephanie, Baroness di Gallotti, of the Pareda-Rosa Grand Opera Co. The entertainment was one of the Occidental's lesser successes, and the usually packed house was barely half-filled. The tall, elegant Stephanie had arrived in Denver in the summer of 1872 with four trunks of silk and lace dresses and the aging baron, Don Carlos. The two had been smuggled out of their native Sardinia by friends after the baron had been sentenced to death for his part in a plot to kill the king. While waiting for a pardon, the exiled couple toured the United States, where Stephanie, a third cousin of Queen Victoria and second cousin of Edward VII sang to keep food in their mouths. Eventually they settled in Denver for the baron's health, and after an unsuccessful attempt to interest Denverites in grand opera at the Occidental, Stephanie found herself entertaining in variety halls and saloons, continuing to wait for the baron's pardon. Finally one afternoon when the baroness returned to their rooms in a Blake Street hotel, she found the pardon—clutched in the lifeless hand of Don Carlos; the excitement had caused his heart to fail. Still young, Stephanie stayed on in Colorado and married a

206

Lined up obligingly in front of the Palace Theatre in this picture, taken about 1880, are some of the members of Denver's sporting fraternity. The disreputable Cricket gambling saloon was not far away, on Blake Street. (A *Denver Tribune* article of 1873 noted that "Charlie Smith, a country lad . . . fell among the 'cappers,' Saturday, and bought up at the Cricket saloon where he lost all his availables.") The Denver Assembly rooms—later the Parlor Minstrel Hall—the Corn Exchange, the Progressive, and the Diana, less noted in history but equally iniquitous, lined Blake Street farther up in the 1500 block (*Denver Public Library Western Collection*).

bartender named Charley Tanner. No longer a baroness, Charley Tanner's wife moved to Leadville where she entertained the miners while her husband tended bar. In 1904, Stephanie, Baroness di Gallotti, cousin of the English royal family and operatic singer who had tried to bring grand opera to a Denver variety hall, her voice broken, her body obese, died destitute in a Leadville hovel.

As might be expected, gambling king Ed Chase built the first of the really elegant Denver gambling mansions, fittingly called "the Palace." Located at 1443–59 Blake, the Palace catered to the finest of Denver's sporting fraternity. Newspaperman Eugene Field, whose Denver fame was based on his practical jokes rather than on the syrupy children's poems he later wrote, was one of the Palace regulars who tried his luck at hop-and-loss, chuck-a-luck, corona, over-and-under-seven, faro, and roulette. H. A. W. Tabor, who played for high stakes and generally lost, was attracted to private games in the upstairs rooms with such big betters as Tom Bowen, the Arkansas carpetbagger who later became Idaho territorial governor, and still later a Colorado senator. Ed Chase once remarked that the amiable Bowen, who liked to josh the girls and play for big money, was "at the same time the finest gentleman and biggest loafer I ever saw."

The Palace had room for 200 players, accommodated by 25 dealers and croupiers. A well-stocked bar, backed by a sixty-foot mirror, insured that their thirst was slaked, and a midnight lunch of roast beef, pork, venison, antelope cutlets, breast of prairie chicken, wild turkey, quail, salads, and sandwiches satisfied their appetites. Not only a gambling hall and saloon, the Palace was a theater as well, seating 750, several of them in curtained boxes where beer sold for one dollar a bottle. Performers were such national favorites as Eddie Foy, Lottie Rogers ("The Leadville Nightingale"), Cora Vane, and the Duncan, Emerson, and Wallace Sisters, as well as Frances Minerva Barbour, whose greatest performance was capturing Ed Chase and becoming his third wife. Despite the quality of its entertainers, the Palace Variety Theatre featured performances as bawdy as those customers had relished at Chase's Progressive and Cricket. A theater program of 1880 bragged in abominable couplets:

> *Palace of Real Pleasure and Voluptuous Art*
> *Where lovely women fascinate the heart*
> *With Nature, Beauty, Music, Song and Dance,*
> *The fancy to enthral and sense entrance.*

Senator Edward O.
Wolcott, whose gam-
bling habits resembled
those of Eastern
multimillionaires
(*Denver Public
Library Western
Collection*).

Despite the fact that Dean Hart of St. John's Cathedral called the Palace a "death-trap to young men, a foul den of vice and corruption" (an obvious endorsement as far as the members of Denver's sporting fraternity were concerned), the Palace continued to attract Denver's most prominent men, none of them more propitious than Senator Edward O. Wolcott, whose betting habits and luck were no less than that of such Eastern big spenders as "Bet-A-Million" Gates. When Wolcott's political critics charged that he had dropped $350,000 (or $22,000, depending on the story) in a single night's faro game at Ed Chase's Palace, the indignant legislator roared, "It's nobody's damned business what I do with my money. Besides, I won it the day before at the races."

Love affairs with Palace showgirls were common in Denver, just as those with Broadway girls would become in New York several decades later. Stage-door Johnnies literally flocked to the dressing rooms of the Palace girls, who accepted the rawer tokens of affection, such as gold dust and small nuggets, with the aplomb of later chorines who raked in furs and diamonds. One of the young men who hung around the Palace, the wayward son of a distinguished Canadian clergyman, succumbed to the charms of dancer Effie Moore. As the happy possessor of the $75,000 capital prize of the Louisiana Lottery, the lover was proud to shower his inamorata with such affectionate trifles as jewels and an ermine cape, but whether the young man worshiped her from afar or found more tangible returns on his generosity is not known. When he found out, however, that Effie was not only married but happily so, he accused her of deception and shot her from his Palace box as she performed on the stage.

Chase and his partner in the Palace, a man named Heatley, sold the theater to the versatile Bat Masterson, who was as fast a hand with cards as with guns. Eventually the gambling hall fell into the hands of Bill Devere, who upheld the Palace's splendidly scandalous reputation with Sunday night "possum and sweet 'tater" suppers served behind locked doors to politicians, businessmen, and Palace chorines. After a heady twenty-five-year operation, the Palace was closed in 1889 during one of Denver's periodic gambling cleanups. The gambling portion of the Palace, at the southeast corner of Fifteenth and Blake, was torn down in 1929; the theater section of the building forty years later.

Ed Chase took advantage of a temporary lull in Denver gambling, provided by one of the city's periodic attempts to clean up, to move his gambling operations to a smart uptown address not far from the plush Windsor Hotel, residence of the flamboyant big-spending gamblers when they were in town. The address was 1609 Larimer, and the building—opened in 1880 as a restaurant, with John Elitch, later proprietor of Elitch Gardens, as chef—had earned a reputation that grew wickeder with each succeeding owner.

Never one to close down his operations (even when the law demanded it), Chase built the present structure around the old one, enclosing the original walls in new ones without so much as a

For nearly half a century Big Ed Chase was Denver's top gambling figure. One of the early argonauts, he opened his first den in the mid-sixties and ran gambling clubs continuously until they were outlawed shortly after the turn of the century. Prematurely gray with steely blue eyes, Chase caused as much scandal with his marital inconsistencies as with his clubs. (*Denver Public Library Western Collection. Courtesy BPOE Lodge #17.*)

minute's interruption in a poker game. He chucked the Arcade's earlier furnishings for fixtures of solid mahogany, glittering chandeliers, French plate-glass mirrors, gold-filled light fixtures, and a thirty-foot bar lighted by a leaded glass skylight in which the traditional tiger loomed in stained glass. In the basement was a large, comfortably furnished hidden room to provide privileged customers with uninterrupted gambling in case of a raid.

The best of Denver's sporting fraternity headquartered at the Arcade—Bat Masterson, the Rincon Kid, and Deadeye Dick. One of the stories Westerners liked best was of an incident supposed to have taken place at the Arcade when Deadeye Dick, playing poker with a group of men one of whom had a patch over his eye, became suspicious of a deal, burnished his six-shooter, and announced, "I ain't mentioning any names, but if someone does any more cheating while I'm here, I'll shoot out his other eye."

Another Arcade habitué was Soapy Smith, Denver con man and inveterate gambler. Whenever he had a few dollars in his pocket, Soapy made his way to the Arcade and played straight through, day and night, until it was all gone. As renowned for his generosity as for his habit of trimming suckers, Soapy once gave Parson Tom Uzzell $1,500 of one-night's winnings ($5,500) to buy Christmas dinners for the poor. Soapy was in a less charitable mood a few years later, however, when he and his brother Bascom shot up the Arcade and several other gaming houses where they had lost money. Bascom was caught, but Soapy escaped to Texas and didn't return for several weeks—and then for only a short time. Along with several other members of Denver's sporting fraternity, he joined the Alaskan gold rush and eventually was shot in a Skagway saloon.

Although Chase no longer sat in his saloon with a shotgun across his knees to discourage rowdiness, his establishments, not always models of decorum, had occasional shootings, one of which kept Denver gossiping for weeks. Jim Moon and Arcade faro dealer Clay Wilson had been good friends until Moon took a shine to Wilson's woman. After several verbal bouts, Moon threatened to kill his rival next time they met, which turned out to be in the

Arcade bar. After a few angry words Moon attempted to draw his gun, but Wilson was too quick for him. He ducked through a door and stalked back in shooting. Although the first bullet pierced Moon's body near his heart, it didn't even stagger him, and he advanced toward Wilson. The second bullet struck Moon a few inches lower, but he kept on, and before Wilson could fire a third shot, Moon was on top of him. Despite Moon's grip, Wilson fired a third shot, hitting Moon in the leg. The fourth bullet, fired without aim, severed Moon's vertebrae and finally killed him. The shooting was the talk of Arcade regulars for weeks; and over six thousand curious Denverites viewed the body the first day it was on display at Albert Brown's undertaking parlor. At a brief trial, Wilson was acquitted on grounds of self-defense.

The biggest gambling game in the Arcade's history, and one of Denver's all-time highest stakes games, took place after Chase had sold the gambling hall to Vaso Chucovich, John J. Hughes, and Charles O. Pierson. Pierson, a former waiter at Charpiot's Restaurant in Denver, had accumulated quite a fortune in Leadville, Aspen, and Glenwood Springs gambling, enough to buy one-third interest in the Arcade and a lot of Colorado real estate besides. An inveterate gambler, Pierson liked to play his own tables, and one particular night attempted to buck the tiger with alarmingly bad luck. Instead of quitting, Pierson approached Hughes about raising the house limit to $10,000. Hughes agreed and opened the play as dealer. With luck still against him Pierson managed to drop $10,000 in twenty minutes, but he still wouldn't quit and offered to put up his interest in the Arcade. Hughes agreed again, and the two jumped into a hack and hightailed it to Chucovich's house at 2:00 A.M., where they awakened their sleeping partner. After two hours of negotiations about the worth of the gambler's share, Pierson and Hughes returned to the Arcade at dawn to continue the game. By that time news of the game's high stakes had spread to Denver's other gambling houses, where the play had closed down to allow the sporting fraternity to gather at the Arcade. The game continued as deal by deal Pierson's share in the Arcade dwindled. When he rose from the table at 10:00 A.M., Pierson had lost a good sum of cash and his interest in the Arcade, and had mortgaged his Glenwood Springs ranch, a total loss of between $50,000 and $100,000.

The Arcade was only one—albeit the most famous one—in a line of iniquitous Larimer Street gambling dens that catered to the sporting fraternity. Next door to it was Murphy's Exchange, called the "Slaughterhouse" for its raucous and frequently bloody happenings. Next to that stood the Gin Mill. Farther down Larimer were the Chicken Coop, Jim Thornton's gambling den, the Missouri House, and Mrs. Anna Guth's Aetna Investment Co. Up on Curtis were the Morgue, the Hog Wallow, and the Clifton House, and there was a scattering of Negro gambling dens on upper Arapahoe and Lawrence.

If the Arcade was the most famous of all these Denver gambling dens of the early 1890's, Murphy's Exchange was the most infamous. Most of Denver's fancy men and pimps gathered there, and at least two sensational deaths revolved around the Slaughterhouse. The first killing involved a pugilist named Clow. In a heinous attempt to murder a man named Marshall, Clow stealthily took the man's gun, unloaded it, and slipped it back into the unwary victim's pocket. Then he attempted to provoke Marshall to draw. In the succeeding fracas, however, it was Clow, not Marshall, who was killed.

The second Slaughterhouse death evoked more comment, probably because it involved Cort Thomson—foot racer, gambler, ladies' man, and the lasting love of Mattie Silks, queen of Denver's red-light district. A prominent member of the sporting fraternity, Cort made his headquarters at Murphy's Exchange because Ed Chase had too much respect for Mattie to let Cort gamble away her money in one of his establishments. While drinking at Murphy's one day, probably on Mattie's money, Cort made the acquaintance of James P. Kerr, owner of the valuable *Breeder and Sportsman* publication in San Francisco. A visitor in Denver, Kerr had been acting queerly for several days and had offered to leave Murphy part of his estate. Murphy replied that he was having hard times, but they weren't that hard. Cort Thomson, however, had no such qualms and not only accepted the offer but hunted up a lawyer to draw the will and paid him with money from Kerr's coat pocket. When Kerr died rather mysteriously several days later, his legatee accompanied the body to San Francisco and made the rounds of the Bay City saloons wearing the dead man's diamond ring.

The circumstances of the death, Cort Thomson's flamboyance, and the loss of a sizable fortune were too much for Kerr's mother and sister, who contested the will. The outcome of the case is unknown since San Francisco court records were destroyed in the 1906 earthquake, but it is probable that Cort either settled out of court for a small sum or was cut out altogether, for after the initial flurry about the inheritance, he never again mentioned the case.

Not long after this, Denver newspapers and churches began a concentrated campaign to abolish gambling in Denver. Although William Byers had attacked gambling regularly since he began publishing the *Rocky Mountain News* in 1859, he had succeeded in bringing about only temporary restraint of Denver operators. But by the mid–1890's the city had begun a major crackdown with the help of the newspapers and occasional independent publishers.

Among the latter was G. N. Scamehorn, who years before had succumbed to "the grim night of hell's dismal way," which had enticed him saying, "We want you. The marble floors in our halls, the frescoed walls, these glittering lights these magnificent paintings, our diamond studs, our fine clothes, our ladies silks and satins . . . ." After losing all trying to buck the tiger, Scamehorn bucked the habit and wrote a righteous if illiterate booklet, *Behind the Scenes or Denver by Gaslight*, exonerating himself.

Scamehorn mournfully bared his soul and those of others to the public in an attempt to discourage young men from following in his footsteps. He described in indignant detail the insides of the nefarious dens: "The first man we see of any prominence is Judge Ballard; the judge is seated at the faro table plugging away his good gold cash in two dollars a shot. See him wipe from his brow the cold perspiration, hear him muttering 'how vain is the hope of man while the foot of the conqueror is on his neck.' "

While not as vivid as Scamehorn, the newspapers did their best

215

to scrape up a few human-interest items in an attempt to agitate their readers. In 1895 the *Rocky Mountain News* ran an article headlined "Gamblers Fleece a Crip . . . Invalid Loses His Little Pile." Despite the seeming refinement of Denver's gambling houses in thirty-five years of operation, they really hadn't progressed at all; quite the opposite. Denver had taken a step backward from that day in 1859 when a Denver House three-card-monte dealer told his audience, "I take no bets from paupers, cripples, or orphan children."

The crowning achievements of Ed Chase's fifty-year Denver gambling spree were two posh uptown clubs, the Inter-Ocean and the Navarre. The Inter-Ocean was originally the splendid Victorian home of Mr. and Mrs. William B. Daniels. Something of a dupe, Daniels was divorced by his wife, who gained possession of the house, later acquired by Chase and partners Robert A. Austin and Barney Boyce. True to tradition, Chase turned the old mansion into a swank gambling den, this one with rich Oriental carpets and excellent paintings. It was the finest gambling casino between Kansas City and San Francisco, with its maze of rooms so confusing to raiders that the evidence usually vanished by the time they found their way through the anterooms to where the actual gambling had been going on. Forty employees served the customers, who were plied with free alcohol as long as they sat at the gaming tables.

For the most part, the Inter-Ocean Club was the most sedate of Chase's many gambling ventures and broke into the news only once, in 1906, when gambler Big Al Hoffses killed an employee, James Thornton—probably the same operator who had run a Larimer Street gambling house—in Chase's office. This was one of Denver's less offensive gambling-hall killings; Hoffses was convicted of voluntary manslaughter and given six to seven years in the state penitentiary. The following year the Inter-Ocean, 1422 Curtis, was turned into a rooming house and later was torn down to make way for a telephone company building.

In the best of traditional Wild West stories, Ed Chase and Vaso Chucovich acquired possession of the ponderous yellow-brick

The Arcade Gambling Hall, 1609–13 Larimer, once a famous Denver den, left, now is a Denver surplus store. Next to it, 1617, Murphy's Exchange, called the "Slaughterhouse" for the blood spilled there, is a citizens' mission. The Gin Mill, center, was once the Manhattan Restaurant, famous for its steaks. The building two doors to the right of it was William H. Jackson's photographic studio.

school building turned Navarre gambling house by winning it from Bob Stockton in a poker game. The cumbersome building at Broadway and Tremont Place was built in 1880 by Professor Joseph Brinker as the Brinker Institute. Brinker died in 1886, and the

A reformed Denver gambler attempted to dissuade young men from bucking the tiger in a book entitled *Behind the Scenes or Denver by Gaslight*, in which he told the story of his own wanton life. Among other things, he listed several ways to fleece a sucker—the gaff (an instrument attached to a ring), roughed cards or strippers, and sanded cards. He also showed—in the above picture—how a young man bilked might retaliate (*Collection of Fred and Jo Mazzulla*).

building first became the Hotel Richelieu—a first-class family hotel with forty-one sleeping rooms, parlors, and reading and smoking rooms—then a moderately successful gambling hall. Not until Chase and Chucovich obtained the building—through fluke or legitimate purchase—did it become the most elegant gambling house in a city known for its flamboyant gambling palaces.

Although Chase obviously was a deft gaming-house proprietor, some of the Navarre's success must be credited to his partner. Vaso Chucovich, Chase's only rival in gambling circles, was a chunky Slav who adorned his bulk with a pink shirt decorated with a huge

The doings were anything but sunshiny in this building at 1851 Larimer, once the Chicken Coop, one of Denver's less reputable gaming establishments. Up the street at 1855 Larimer was a gambling hall run by James Thornton, and farther on, at 1859, another operated by Fred Koch.

diamond stuck in the front. Despite his unlikely appearance, Chucovich was a power in Denver politics for years and a personal friend of Mayor Robert W. Speer, who eventually closed Denver's gambling halls.

The two together—Chase and Chucovich—were an unbeatable combination in gambling-house proprietorship and made of the Navarre, named for the lusty Henry of Navarre, the finest gambling establishment in their part of the West.

If a gentleman came to the Navarre alone, suggested an early-day promotion booklet, he might wander into the white and crystal bar and order a drink while he gazed at a life-size rendition of *After the Bath*. Later he might sup in the Renaissance-style upstairs dining room with wreaths painted on the ceiling and animal pictures on the paneled walls. "If Madame is with you and you desire privacy," noted the brochure, the gentleman would enter by the discreet north door and spirit his inamorata up the stairs to a private dining room. Or perhaps if Madame were presentable enough, the gentleman would take her to one of the high-backed leather settees in the grill room where call-button service prevented indiscreet interruptions or summoned a waiter when the gentleman desired "broiled things and glasses that 'clink' suggestions of cooling, cheering draughts."

All the Navarre's rooms were handsomely furnished with velvet carpets, plush furniture, and Gothic-framed "figure pieces" entitled *The Lorelei, Morning, Night, Little Egypt, Whispering Love*, and *Trilby*. Two other paintings were perhaps better known. One, *The Parlor Match*, shows a Negro family waiting for an explosion as Papa lights the first match they've ever seen. The other, *Bucking the Tiger*, shows a high-stakes game in a Western saloon, one of the finest pictures of a gambling scene ever painted.

Chase's and Chucovich's predecessor, Stockton, originally designed the Navarre for the well-heeled spender who appreciated not only gambling but good food and privacy. An early promotion booklet promised:

In this day of great caravansaries, the man of imagination who

The Inter-Ocean Club, 1422 Curtis, was once the extravagantly Victorian home of William B. Daniels, who started Daniels & Fisher. Mountain Bell's office stands on the site today (*Collection of Fred and Jo Mazzulla*).

really understands how to be happy, sighs for the simpler inns of the olden times, where two or three good fellows could "dram up" together, fill a bumper, sing a song, and eat a good dinner, without being the target of a hundred eyes; without being put out of a great glittering dining room as a freak.

Luckily for our modern mortality, there is in every town a cozy inn, if one only knows where to find it. Denver's cozy inn is in plain sight, not hidden away in a dark alley like so many of them in the older cities . . . . A modest yellow brick house it is, looking a dwelling prepared for a wedding with its awning leading up from the curb; a modest sign in black and gold tells you that this is the "Navarre . . . ."

This was a set-up designed indeed to appeal to Chase and the diamond-fronted Chucovich, from the cellar, with its Amontillado

221

The club featured a series of gaming rooms. This handsomely decorated room, shown in the palmiest days, was decorated with velvet portieres at the windows and velvet carpets on the floors (*Collection of Fred and Jo Mazzulla*).

sherry and private tunnel connecting the club with the Brown Palace Hotel across the street, to the upstairs Gentlemen's Private Club where the big spenders operated.

Unlike most of Chase's establishments, the Navarre was the picture of decorum, although that may be as much a credit to its

Probably intended as the house's ballroom, this well-furnished gaming room under the cupola skylight was generously fitted with gambling apparatus. Conveniently placed spittoons and the bar at one end of the room took care of a gentleman's other needs (*Collection of Fred and Jo Mazzulla*).

short life as a gambling house as to any conscious effort of Chase's. The Navarre was closed not long after the turn of the century when Denver finally outlawed gambling houses. It eventually became the Denver Republican Club headquarters, then a fine restaurant.

223

ESTABLISHED 1877.

Platoons of Brinker boys never marched about these twin classroom-dormitory buildings envisioned by Professor Brinker in 1877 because they never were built. The professor did manage to erect one structure, however, similar if less elegant. Its many classrooms and small dormitory rooms made it an ideal hotel and later a discreet gambling club. Today the Navarre, the building is little changed from the original structure, erected in 1880 (*Denver Public Library Western Collection*).

Chucovich's friend Mayor Speer, aided by the crusading zeal of the *Rocky Mountain News*, was responsible for shutting down the Navarre and other Denver gambling houses in the early 1900's,

One of the finest gambling pictures ever painted, *Bucking the Tiger*, which hung in the Navarre for many years, shows a group of men concentrating on a high-stakes game. Old-time gamblers have been unable to explain the sign on the wall, "$25 and $50 for $100 Change in" (*Collection of Fred and Jo Mazzulla*).

and the Navarre's gambling died quietly, without a whimper, at the appointed time. A few hours before Denver gambling became illegal, the *News* editor (a successor of Byers') who had spurred much of his paper's campaign against gambling, surprisingly something of a Navarre regular, wandered into the club and won $200. "That's adding insult to injury," Chase told him wrathfully. "You not only close me up, but you top it off by winning my money."

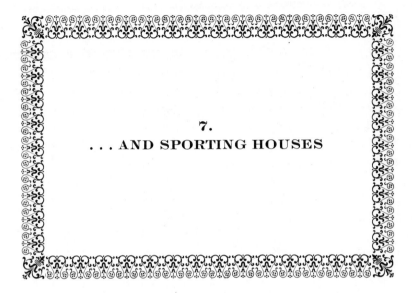

7.

. . . AND SPORTING HOUSES

I<small>F HE WASN'T TOO METICULOUS</small> (and nobody ever claimed he was),
an 1859 sourdough on the Cherry Creek might find his pleasure
with an amiable, unwashed young Indian woman in the privacy of
a tipi thoughtfully provided by her husband, who was only too
happy to collect a few coins for his wife's labor; still, most of the
city's early transients yearned to be clasped in white arms, whose
hue seemingly whitewashed a multitude of sins. Fortunately for
the first settlers—whose lust was not only for gold—where there
were money and men who needed satisfaction, there soon were
women happy to exchange one for the other.

It was only fitting in a town that delighted in depravity that the
city's legendary first madam, the high-styled Ada LaMont, was
really a minister's wife, who took her light from under the bushel,
shaded it in red, and hung it up on a shack in Indian Row. Shortly
after the first settlers had arrived in Denver, Ada had headed west
with her husband to teach the Gospel. The nineteen-year-old

227

preacher's wife, whose chastity already had been impugned with stories that she had been a bareback rider, was deserted by her groom, a young man more zealous in his pursuit of a lady of doubtful reputation on the wagon train than in spreading the Word. The two took off, leaving Ada destitute. A shrewd young lady, Ada realized the financial disadvantages of Bible teaching and shocked the solicitous members of the wagon train when she reached Denver City by announcing that she had decided to set up a bagnio on the banks of the South Platte. Ada dealt in a then-scarce commodity, and a year later, to accommodate the demands of her public, she moved uptown to a larger two-story house on Arapahoe. There she operated for ten years on a few chosen tenets of the Ten Commandments: She might commit adultery, she might covet her neighbor's husband, but she didn't take the Lord's name in vain, steal, or roll a drunk. Also for poor enterprising Ada, her story ended in tragedy. Ten years after she arrived in Denver, a friend found her husband's skeleton and a Bible, the bride's wedding gift, on the prairie. The shock was too much for Ada, who started drinking, lost her house, and ended in the gutter.

During her more successful years, however, Ada LaMont dealt in a profitable business, and it wasn't long before she had competition, not merely from the tenants of Indian Row but from the tents of Auraria and Arapahoe Street. Before long Denver was well endowed with brothels set up not only along the familiar alleys of Blake and McGaa but out across the Ferry Street Bridge in the Highlands, where John Kingston and "a wretched woman ripe for the bottomless pit, whose only known name is Aunt Betsy" sold the services of five of the "most brazen-faced journey-women harlots, that ever walked the pave of any city." Another area that lured the sinful was out near "five points," just above the Union Freight Depot, which "from the general asperity of the denizens there," the police called "Vinegar Hill." As yet uncivilized, Denver City refused to keep its harlots in a proscribed area but spread them across the city for the convenience of its men. Like gold, love at the Cherry Creek was where you found it.

Long before Denver's bonanza kings developed a taste for

French companions, imported champagne, and hundred-dollar-a-night revels, the city had a well-organized row. Brothels were prominent, although most men were satisfied for a dollar at the city's cribs, gathered as loosely as their occupants' morals along Market* and annexed onto a side street known as the Blue Row, where the girls charged only a dime. Nondescript one-story shacks, the cribs were nearly indistinguishable from one another except for the girl's name—"Rosie" or "LaVerne" or "Dixie Lee"—painted on the front. Generally composed of a front and a back room, one for receiving, the other for working (or else one was used for business purposes, the other for living quarters), each crib was cheaply furnished with a washstand, an iron bed spread with a gaudy coverlet, and sometimes the homey touch of a few religious pictures on the wall. Generally, a girl solicited from the door, although sometimes she left the curtains open so that an interested customer willing to wait his turn could windowshop while she was working.

Occasionally a larger building along the row provided a nest of cubicles where the girls plied their trade. Rickety steps led up from the street to a squalid hallway so narrow that two persons could barely pass, and in case of fire a rush of three or four would have blocked escape. Between what an early newspaper called its "insect haunted walls," wretched creatures operated in dank rooms, selling their squalid selves for paltry sums to men grim enough to enter, debased enough to need what those pitiful creatures sold. This was not the expensive, glittering life of the demi-mondaine, so popular in later historical accounts, but the sordid, wretched existence of a prostitute.

While the crib girls were the working masses of Denver's soiled doves and the first ones to ease the cares of the Cherry Creek prospectors, they were scorned by the girls of the parlor houses, although many of the higher-class bagnio employees ended their days in the cribs. Working for a promoter was infinitely more desirable

*Originally called McGaa then Holladay then Market, the street, to avoid confusion, will be referred to from now on as Market, although that name was not adopted until well into the street's infamy. A different street-numbering system existed until the mid–1880's, but all addresses given are based on present designations.

229

than being in business for oneself. The crib cubicles so hated and feared by the parlor-house girls were rank and stale from smoke and liquor and lust. The girls were onerous and weak from too much drink or dope or just depravity. By the time a prostitute reached the cribs, she usually was unfit for anything but prostitution. She was no longer a soiled dove; she was a whore.

Murder and theft in the cribs were frequent; suicide, especially at Christmastime, was so common it rated only scant notice in the newspapers. An 1886 newspaper account going into more detail than usual about a crib-girl suicide described the woman's room, likening it to a slum in a Dickens novel:

> The room, it is said, is only a sample of the rest in the ricketty [sic] old row. The walls and ceiling were absolutely black with smoke and dirt, excepting where old, stained newspapers had been pasted on them—on the ceiling, to exclude rain and melting snow, and on the walls, to cover up spots from which the plastering had fallen. The floor was rickety and filthy. Around the walls were disposed innumerable unwashed and battered tin cooking utensils, shelves, for the most part laden with dust, old clothing, which emitted a powerful effluvium, hung from nails here and there; or tumble-down chairs, a table of very rheumatic tendency, on which were broken cups, plates and remnants of food, were scattered all over its surface. An empty whisky bottle and pewter spoon or two. In one corner and taking up half the space of the den was the bedstead strongly suggestive of a bountiful crop of vermin, and on that flimsy bed lay the corpse of the suicide, clad in dirty ragged apparel, and with as horrid a look on her begrimmed, pallid features as the surroundings presented. No one of her neighbors in wretchedness had had the sense to open either of the two little windows in the room to admit pure air, hence the atmosphere was sickeningly impure and almost asphixiating. "My God!" exclaimed Coroner McHatton, used as he is to similar scenes and smells in his official capacity, "Isn't this awful?"

Like the rest of Denver City, the town's parlor houses were fussy Victorian dwellings unrestrained by any semblance of good taste, lavishly adorned outside, inside overflowing with preponderance of bad design—mirrored walls and ceilings that reflected rich woodwork, grand pianos, and Louis XIV furniture, with

As a satisfied patron strides up the street, the girl at 2130 peers about for another customer. These cribs, located in the 2100 block of Market Street were just a block uptown from the parlor houses, and considerably nicer than some of the shacks inhabited by other girls on the row (*Denver Public Library Western Collection*).

Some of Denver's more affluent crib girls lived in the Batione Hotel, 1720 Larimer, built in 1881 by the respectable Mrs. C. I. Batione. The cribs were cold and dreary besides being a constant reminder to a girl of her profession, and a hotel not only was a nicer place to live but safer. Denver's row suffered at least one murderous rampage when a killer, probably posing as a customer, knifed several prostitutes. A number of Denver's row girls left town while others took a leave of absence and moved into hotels.

A couple of Belle's girls pose in front of the house before going to work. Madam Birnard operated this house at 518 Market (renumbered 1952 Market) in the 1880's and 1890's (*Denver Public Library Western Collection*).

ottomans for the girls, grouped on swank linoleum carpets. The finest rooms in the houses were the reception rooms where the girls, or "boarders" as the madams liked to call their employees, gathered to meet their callers. Some of the houses featured banquet rooms, which doubled as dining rooms for the girls during off hours, along with kitchens, wine cellars in the basements, and of course a multitude of bedrooms on the second floor. Furnished much as the cribs were if somewhat more affluently, the boarders' rooms were fitted with iron or brass beds, dressers, commodes and slop jars, trunks, and sometimes personal effects—dolls, holy pictures, and tranquil scenes. Some of the girls displayed photographs of themselves, which they sold as remembrances. To the universal gloom of all, the windows were barred to prevent customers from escaping across the rooftops without paying or to keep the girls from doing a little independent business.

No one knows who opened the first Market Street parlor house, and indeed, that is the sort of question only historians quibble about. But anyone who is interested knows that the most elegant house in Denver's red-light district, an area known affectionately by the roués and fobs from Saratoga Springs to the Gold Coast, was the House of Mirrors, built by Jennie Rogers and reigned over by the queen of Market Street, Mattie Silks.

Market had long been established as Denver's parlor-house district when Jennie Rogers built her stunning house. For many years young ladies had romped with their callers to the tunes the professor banged out on the grand pianos in the stately two-story houses along the row. Nor was Jennie herself new to Market Street. Leeah J. Fries, as she was known legally, came to Denver in 1879 flush with parlor-house triumph in St. Louis and immediately purchased a bagnio from Mattie Silks, 2009 Market Street, a two-story brick with decorative windows and cast-iron rooftop trim, one of the few parlor houses still standing on Market and the only one with a wisp of former opulence. Jennie bought the house in January, 1880, for $4,600 and turned it into one of the plushest parlor houses in the district. So popular was it, in fact, that she sold it only four years later in order to build a more substantial

Most famous sex palace in all the Rocky Mountain gold-rich country was Jennie Rogers' House of Mirrors, later Mattie Silks's establishment, and here, in this painting by Herndon Davis in the 1930's, a Buddhist church. As if to atone for its sins, the House of Mirrors today is a warehouse (*Denver Public Library Western Collection*).

bagnio at 1950 Market. Dominated by the Turkish Room, one of three first-floor parlors, Jennie's second Denver house, a three-story building, featured a ballroom, a dining room, servants' quarters, a wine cellar, and fifteen bedrooms. Probably the finest house on the row until Jennie built the inimitable House of Mirrors, 1950 Market was leased to Jennie's friend Etta Kelly in 1904 and sold to her in 1911, after Jennie's death, for a paltry sum.

The six-foot, raven-haired Jennie was at the apex of her career when she blackmailed a prominent Denver citizen into building her

House of Mirrors. Jennie, like all Denver's madams, was scrupulous about keeping the names of her customers secret; blackmailing a patron was akin to dishonor among thieves. But happily, the man who financed Jennie's lavish brothel was persuaded to put up the money to conceal something other than what Jennie might have known about him professionally. According to a former St. Louis detective who was Jennie's lover, the Denver gentleman had married a young woman who had then disappeared suddenly, leaving him free to marry the wealthy wife of his employer. The woman had divorced her husband to wed the penniless young man. The second marriage was the beginning of a successful financial career for the Denver gentleman, and he had only lately turned to politics. Jennie and her lover threatened to accuse the man of murdering his first wife (and, indeed, there was a chance he had, said Jennie's lover), insist that the body was buried in the back yard, and perhaps even make sure that a skeleton would be there to be found. Even if no evidence of foul play was discovered, the man's political career would be ruined by the scandal.

As Jennie's lover had reckoned, the old boy fell for the ploy and put up $17,000 to save his reputation. Jennie hired architect William Quayle, erstwhile designer of Trinity Methodist Church, to draw plans for the house that would be admired by the sporting life of the entire West. Built in 1888, the most famous sex palace in the Rocky Mountains was three stories of cut stone lavishly decorated with faces and phallic symbols. In the gable a buxom sculpture of Jennie presided over the house, while from the third-story façade below peered the faces of a gentleman, a fat woman, a young lady, and a lecherous old man—said to be the cuckolded employer, his wife, the Denver gentleman's first wife, and the gentleman himself, grown fat.

Called the House of Mirrors for the lavish mirrors lining the reception walls and ceiling, the brothel was as showy inside as out, with Oriental rugs on parquet floors, a crystal chandelier in an eight-foot circular mirror hanging from the reception room ceiling, plate-glass sliding doors opening into a ballroom furnished with a grand piano and golden chairs, and a walnut staircase leading past prints of horses, Jennie's addiction, to the second-floor bedrooms. A heavily veiled plate-glass window overlooked Market; all other windows had the inevitable half-inch iron bars. The entire cost was $780 more than the blackmailed man had given Jennie, but after a little more prodding, he picked up the tab on the additional expense, too.

In order to handle the increased patronage the House of Mirrors brought, Jennie connected it with 1946 Market, which she furnished to resemble a harem, and probably linked that to her old house at 1950. Jennie Rogers and her girls were the elite of the demimonde in the House of Mirrors, where they entertained the country's most prominent men with champagne (five dollars a split), dancing (a gentleman always tipped the orchestra), and equally expensive upstairs activity. Although there never was any question about the principal commodity of 1942 Market, many of the house's customers were wealthy gentlemen who came just to be entertained, to ogle the girls all the while sipping Jennie's expensive wines. Regularly the state legislature, meeting in the Barclay Block a short distance away, adjourned in the afternoons to Jennie's bordello for a few hours of frolic. There was little doubt that Jennie was queen of the red-light district when she opened the House of Mirrors, although she didn't reign as long or as well as her rival Mattie Silks, who purchased the famous house at 1942 Market in 1911, after Jennie's death. By then Denver's red-light district was on the wane, although the madams weren't aware of it. Mattie refurbished the house and proclaimed her ownership with "M. Silks" spelled in tiles at the entrance, but she operated the bagnio for only a few years. The house was sold in 1919 and again in 1929 to become a Buddhist church. In 1948 the famous House of Mirrors was stripped of its former grandeur, masked with a coat of stucco, and turned into a warehouse.

Old-timers like to quibble, as old-timers are supposed to, about who really ruled Denver's Market Street, but historians, whose information, alas, nearly always is secondhand at best, generally give the crown to Mattie Silks, the curly-haired Denver darling who liked to brag that she hadn't worked her way up but had entered

Mattie Silks, who originally owned this fashionable bawdy house, sold it in 1880 to Jennie Rogers. Despite its squalor, this house is the only one left on Market Street with any class to its appearance.

the business as a madam. Mattie arrived in Denver City in the mid–1870's after a successful tent tour of the mining camps. Equipped with several lovely boarders and a tent big enough for business, Mattie discarded the canvas structure in Denver for a more substantial building on Market Street. Soon she was installed in a classy bagnio, a sophisticated two-story brick with long windows shrouded in awnings, later connected with a two-story stone house next door. Mattie ran the two houses, 1916–22 Market, for nearly thirty years, until she moved into the House of Mirrors. Although there may have been some question about who was queen exactly when, there never was any doubt that the Mesdames Rogers and Silks together were on top for the duration of the red-light era in Denver. They were shrewd businesswomen, the tall beauty and the plump dumpling, who made as much from peddling wine as women. Loyal to their customers and kind to their girls, the two had a weakness for fine horses and fancy men, both of which they kept. Married several times apiece, they were ruefully aware they had to keep the store going in order to put up their men in style.

It wasn't lack of competition but good management that kept Jennie and Mattie on top as queens of the demimonde. There were plenty of aspirants ready to replace one or the other. Denver's *Red Book*, issued in 1892 for the convenience of the Knights Templar holding a conclave in Denver, carried advertisements of half a dozen madams anxious to please the traveler or hometown boy. Belle Birnard operated fourteen rooms with twelve boarders at 1952 Market. Jennie Holmes had three parlors, two ballrooms, and a poolroom, nicely decorated with fifteen girls. Blanche Brown, at the corner of Twentieth and Market, advertised "Lots of Boarders—All the Comforts of Home," and Minnie A. Hall, down the street at 1950, boasted thirty rooms, five parlors and Mikado parlor, and twenty boarders.

In the interest of historical accuracy the addresses, alas, are useless as a present-day directory—the following is a list of the houses that stood on Denver's two-block-long row. Interspersed with cribs and saloons, the bagnios were concentrated on Market, with a few on the side streets or uptown on Arapahoe and Curtis. Supplied by befogged memories more concerned with remembering events than addresses and confused by frequent changes of

239

ownership along with a new street name and numbering system, the list makes no pretense of being complete:

1916 Market: Owned by Mattie Silks for forty years, this house was opened in the late 1870's and continued to operate as a parlor house for thirty years.

1922 Market: Connected with 1916 by a passageway, this was another of M. Silks's houses.

1942 Market: Originally a frame brothel run by Eva Lewis, 1942 Market was the site of the West's most splendid sex palace, Jennie Rogers' House of Mirrors. Later a Buddhist church, it now is a warehouse.

1950 Market: Built in 1884, this bagnio was presided over by Jennie Rogers and was one of Denver finest houses until she built the House of Mirrors.

1952 Market: A stylish two-story Victorian house, this brothel was run by Belle Birnard (fourteen rooms, five parlors, music and dance halls, twelve boarders, "Strictly First-Class in Every Respect"). Later it was operated by Leona de Camp, a House of Mirrors girl who made her way up.

1962 Market: "In it were many scenes that called police attention to the vicinity," wrote Gene Fowler, reporter for the *Denver Post*, in an article about Denver's recently closed red-light district. But he did not make clear whether the site housed bagnio or bar.

1901 Market: The Monte Carlo Saloon, favorite gathering place of *maquereaux* and fancy men.

1905 Market: A crib.

1913–17 Market: The Circus, a three-story building, was a haunt of Denver roués who paid a buck on Saturday nights to see a lewd show.

1923 Market: When Eva Lewis left 1942 Market to let Jennie Rogers build her famous House of Mirrors on the site, she moved to this address, across the street from Mattie Silks.

1937 Market: Wallace's Saloon.

1943 Market: Originally 433 Holladay, this was Lizzie Preston's house. Baby Doe led a raid on Lizzie's house to gather material for divorce proceedings against her husband Harvey Doe. She found it.

1957–59 Market: A bagnio operated by Jennie Rogers early in her career.

2000 Market: The Alcazar, bar, backrooms, and burlesque, where beer was served to "hop-head, rounder and sport," wrote Gene Fowler.

2014–20 Market: A two-story brownstone mansion with two entrances, this house was operated in the 1880's by Jennie Rogers and later leased to Lillis Lovell. Lois Lovell, one of the girls in her sister's house, was wildly in love with a prominent young Denver businessman who had attempted to persuade her to marry him. Lois had refused, knowing her profession would ruin her lover. After pleading in vain, the man left the city on a business trip, and to the whistle of his train pulling out of the station, Lois shot herself in her room at 2020 Market. A week later her lover returned, jubilant with the idea the two could marry and move away to a place where no one knew Lois' background. Told she had killed herself, the young man insisted on being taken to her grave at Riverside Cemetery, where he fell on the fresh mound of earth and blew out his brains. The bagnio later was run as the Baldwin Inn, the "House of a Thousand Memories," by the statuesque Verona Baldwin, a colorful madam who claimed she had been ruined by her cousin, wealthy California eccentric Lucky Baldwin. During prohibition the building was turned into a furniture warehouse; in 1926 it was razed.

2062 Market: A saloon.

2001 Market: Run by Fay Stanley, this address was a fancy two-story brothel with an entrance on Twentieth Street.

2005 Market: The Fashion, a smart bagnio, run by Mesdames Blanche Brown, Rose Lovejoy, and Belle London.

2009 Market: Jennie Rogers, who had nearly as many houses as her girls had customers in an evening, purchased this bagnio in 1880 from Mattie Silks. One of the three or four parlor houses still standing on Market Street and now a warehouse, it has an air of having seen better days.

241

2015 Market: This address, now Cathay Post, American Legion #185, was operated by Mesdames Verona Baldwin, Minnie Hall, and Jennie Holmes (twenty-three rooms, three parlors, two ballrooms, poolroom, fifteen boarders, "Everything Correct"). It was owned for a time by Madam Amy Basset, a genteel lady from Kentucky whose son was graduated from Yale.

It was coincidental, although it would have pleased Jennie Rogers, that her death marked the demise of the Market Street bagnios. Far from the striking beauty she had once been, Jennie died in 1910, only a year before Robert Speer, who had put the city's gamblers out of business, closed the cribs. Nearly three hundred women were thrown out of work in 1911 by a law aimed not so much at their poor besodden selves as at the *maquereaux* who lived off them. The law allowed the parlor houses to remain open, to the delight of Mattie Silks, who had just acquired Jennie's House of Mirrows, but the days were numbered even for the aging monarch of Market. The next year, 1912, Denver's mayor ordered the city's red-light district cleaned up and many of the cribs along the row torn down. A year later, police attempted to close even the most circumspect of sex palaces, but they merely dispersed the prostitutes temporarily among the city's hotels, cafes, and rooming houses, and within a few months the girls had made their way back to Market and the madams who attempted to reopen. Although Denver enacted stiffer and stiffer laws to discourage parlor houses and prostitutes, it took a concentrated effort by the officers of the U.S. Army to shut down the most famous sin street in the West, much to the dismay of the regulars. And the army didn't do it until 1918. Mattie Silks, queen almost to the end, sick and tired, although she had more than a dozen years left to live, quit the street in 1915 and retired to a demure cottage at 2635 Lawrence.

Like Mattie, the more astute madams realized that the party was over, and shortly after Mattie left, they, too, drew the velvet drapes and locked the doors that had stood wide open for forty years. And when the madams left, the girls, like their morals, scattered with every wind and made their way to various parts of

One of the operators of this bordello was a lady from Kentucky whose
son was a Yale man.

the city. Never again was Denver to have a row. Market Street
was closed. The most infamous row in the West, "Hell's Swift
Alley . . . bounded on the north by stumbling virtue, on the south
by wrecked hopes, on the east by the miserably gray dawn of
shame and on the west by the sunset of dissipation," as Gene
Fowler wrote the year the street shut down, was converted to a
warehouse district whose bawdier times are remembered today by
only a few very old men.

8.
THE CHERRY CREEK AT PLAY

CULTURE CAME QUICKLY to Denver City. It rambled into town past the go-backs late in September, 1859, with Colonel Charles R. Thorne and his troupe of players, who had come at the urging of General Larimer to entertain the gold-seekers. They opened with *Cross of Gold* or *The Maid of Croissey* a week later, October 3, 1859, to the shattering of glasses and the shouts of gamblers, on the second floor of Libeus Barney's Apollo Hotel on Larimer Street.

Finished only a couple of weeks before Thorne arrived, the Apollo Hall and Billiard Saloon was advertised as the first floored, finished, and conveniently arranged public house of first-class style in Denver. The second-floor meeting hall was the best in the combined cities of Auraria and Denver, although it had neither ceiling nor plaster and only a dozen candles to serve as theater footlights. Despite its physical drawbacks and the exorbitant one dollar per person charge, nearly 350 miners and a few ladies crowded onto

245

Apollo Hall, second from left, was the Cherry Creek's first attempt at legitimate theater. Opened in 1859, it specialized in spoofs, melodrama, and high-styled tragedy. (*Denver Public Library Western Collection. Photograph by William C. Chamberlain.*)

the rough benches to see Colonel Thorne and his star, the virginal Mlle Rose Haydee. The rattling of billiards and raucous songs from below punctuated the performances, and occasionally drunks in the audience took part, but none of this disturbed the miners.

A year after the Apollo opened, the audience was no politer. Journalist Albert D. Richardson reported attending *La Tour de Nesle* at the Apollo in 1860. Gaultier agonizingly asked concerning his murdered relative:

"Where, O where is my brother?"
A sepulchral voice from the midst of the house, answered:

246

"I am thy brother!"

The spectators supposed it a part of the play, but discovering that the response came from a favorite candidate for Congress greeted it with cheer after cheer.

Queen Marguerite with due horror gave the exclamation:

"Then I am lost indeed!"

A miner, directly in front of the stage, responded emphatically: "You bet."

Despite Thorne's immediate success at the Apollo, the Thespian deserted the Denver stage after only two weeks of performances. The company went by default to Mlle Rose, who organized it into Haydee's Star Company. With her charming air and elegance as a danseuse, Rose Haydee was star of her troupe playing opposite the "inimitable" Mike J. Dougherty, popular low comedian. Rose's half-sisters, Flora and Louise Wakely, made up most of the rest of the company. The girls' mother had permanently ensconced herself in Denver with her husband, George Wakely, Denver's first photographer, who opened the Ambrotype Gallery directly across the street from the Apollo.

Under Rose's direction the troupe reopened the Apollo in early November, 1859, and a month later performed the first dramatic production from the pen of a Denver playwright. Entitled *Skatara, the Mountain Chieftain*, the epic production was written by Army Captain A. B. Steinberger as a lofty tribute to the newly created Jefferson Territory that encompassed Colorado. The four-act tragedy was a flop with the miners, however, until Mlle Haydee burlesqued it in a spoof, *Skatterer, the Mountain Thief*.

The Haydee Star Company presented the only legitimate theater in the Pikes Peak country until September, 1860, when John S. ("Jack") Langrishe brought his acting troupe from Fort Laramie to Denver. After a few successful performances he joined forces with Mike Dougherty, hero of the Haydee Star Troupe. Rose had run away with a Central City gambler, to the despair of the miners up and down Gregory Gulch, and enamored with domestic life, she was happy to let Dougherty and Langrishe take over the Apollo. After several performances in Denver, the two men, out-

247

standing actors, set off for a grand tour of the mining camps, and when they returned, they discovered that Denver had become enthralled with entertainers.

No matter what the entertainment, it made money for Apollo owner Libeus Barney, who estimated his profit the first few months at $50 a day. Even when the hall was closed, Barney managed to scrape up a few dollars in gold dust. One morning, with a turkey wing and a whisk broom, he swept up $13.56 in gold from the Apollo floor, along with a note:

DEAREST WILLIE

My husband started for the Park yesterday, and, if agreeable, please call around at ten o'clock this evening.

Yours anxiously,
NELLY

P.S. Knock at the back door three times. N.

To compete successfully for the sophisticated theatergoers crowding into Denver, the partners had to close the Apollo periodically for repairs. The most extensive remodeling was finished in October, 1861, when the building was lengthened thirty feet, part of the upper floor was cut out to leave room for a gallery, and all new gold-and-white decorations, worth $2,000, were installed. Despite the changes, the remodeled Apollo, that "perfect gem of a house," with its dress circle, drawing-room atmosphere, and the finest stage west of Chicago, wasn't good enough for Denver City, and the partners leased it in mid–1862 to the Methodist Episcopal Church for services while they built the Denver Theatre. The new venture was very successful, but the two men soon parted. Dougherty died of drink a few years later; Langrishe eventually opened the Leadville Tabor Opera House; the delightful Rose gave a number of final farewell performances and eventually succumbed to domestic life. The Apollo dragged on for a while, and sometime after it was abandoned by even the Methodists, the hall was torn down.*

*The section on the Apollo Theatre is adapted from Sandra Dallas, *Gold and Gothic* (Denver, Lick Skillet Press, 1967).

248

The immense, barn-size Denver Theatre, located just a few doors from the Pacific House, better known as the Broadwell House, lacked the plush decor of Denver's later theaters. It also lacked the audiences (*Denver Public Library Western Collection*).

The Denver Theatre, acquired by Jack Langrishe and the inimitable Mike Dougherty (whose name was as faithfully preceded by the adjective as if he had been christened with it), was a hulking barn of a building with an entrance that looked like a stable door. Built by a group of Easterners using Colorado capital and donated city land, the Platte Valley Theatre, as it originally was called, took a full six months to complete. Despite the cheap materials used and the preponderance of somebody else's cash, the backers ran out of money before the theater was finished and gave a couple of ice-cream suppers to supplement the building fund. They didn't bring in much, but the theater opened anyway, in October, 1861, with a generous bill—*Richard III, The Devil's In the Room* (a comedy enlivened by variety acts), and a serious poem recited by the theater manager, all in a single night's performance.

The scarcity of money for building was matched, alas, by the equally sparse revenue from ticket sales, and the theater closed for the winter for lack of business. Possibly because the scheduled theater performances failed to attract patrons, several plays were given under the guise of "benefits," the most notable of them being *Where Is the Governor?*, a satire about Governor Gilpin's trip to Washington. Suffering financial embarrassment equal to that of the theater the governor had gone to the nation's Capital in an attempt to convince the Treasury Department to recognize drafts he had issued to local merchants to equip the First Regiment of Colorado Volunteers, the territory's Civil War effort.

After a noticeably bad season, the Platte Valley was sold to Langrishe and Dougherty for $2,500 and renamed the Denver Theatre. The two presented an ambitious program of entertainment ranging from high tragedy to burlesque with occasional stereopticon shows and concerts. One of their most touted programs featured a reenactment of the Battle of Charleston climaxed by a salvo of cannon fire from a real cannon followed by the "Anvil Chorus," pounded out on six anvils loaned for the occasion by a stage-struck blacksmith. Another popular program was *Pat Casey's Night Hands*, a satire inspired by a preposterous Central City illiterate whose sudden wealth produced hysterically funny aristocratic airs.

250

Casey couldn't read or write but bragged he used ten "lid" pencils a day figuring his accounts. A favorite story about Casey which made the rounds of Denver circles was about a lunch break at one of his mines:

"How many of youse are there?" Casey hollered down the mine shaft one noon.

"Five," came up the answer.

Casey attempted a moment of concentrated figuring then brightened and yelled, "Well, half of youse come up for lunch."

The Casey satire was an immense success in Denver, but when Dougherty and Langrishe took their play to Central City, Casey's stomping grounds, they met with opposition not only from Pat but from his hired hooligans, the night hands themselves. Casey sent his crew to the theater to stop the performace, but Dougherty, in a masterly stroke, invited Central City's local guards to attend the theater, armed, as his guests, and the play came off as scheduled.

The Denver Theatre not only looked like a barn, it was built like one. "The coldest thing about the theatre," ran a popular remark, "is the inside of it." The proprietors attempted to brighten the atmosphere with a new backdrop of Lord Byron to replace the original set, an inspired complex of a peculiar mountain, a building that looked like a Chinese pagoda with Roman Catholic Church overtones, and a man, in the position of a soldier loading a musket, poling a whale boat. Little that the partners could do, however, could make the Denver Theatre more attractive. Langrishe eventually took over the business, shortly before Dougherty expired in an attack of delirium tremens; and despite a statewide slump in theater attendance, he and later owners managed to put on a creditable number of performances. One of them was a lecture by P. T. Barnum, managed by Professor Owen J. Goldrick, who collected a $247 profit from the till while P. T., who was one of Colorado's biggest suckers, came away with a paltry $75, to the undisguised glee of the *Rocky Mountain News*, which couldn't refrain from commenting.

The theater was sold several times to intermittently successful owners who presented such attractions as Artemus Ward and

251

Cassius Clay, but with each succeeding owner, the Denver became grimier. Finally, under the name of the Wigwam, the stable-like Denver Theatre burned down in 1873. The corner on which it stood at Sixteenth and Lawrence long since has been improved with the building now occupied by the American Furniture Company.

Despite the fact that theater business in Denver was in the doldrums, the *Rocky Mountain News* angled for a new hall, with unsubtle suggestions that a better building would bring a bigger crowd. "If our people would patronize the drama they must needs pack themselves into a dingy and dilapidated old shell. Perhaps, however, we ought to evince more charity, especially toward the aged, and not fling our innuendoes at the unpretentious pile, the old Denver Theatre. The substitution of a more suitable building for purposes theatrical would be hailed as an especially desirable improvement."

Although the *News* was loath to reveal it, Denver City was essentially lowbrow—or more accurately, its intellectual taste was nearly in the gutter—and Denver itself, surprisingly enough, is equally reluctant to admit that William N. Byers, the *News* editor, despite his one deflating love affair, was a pompous bore and a prude. With the blatant theater-worship of a shopgirl, the city lionized the members of visiting acting troupes, who saw the social elite of other cities mostly from the wrong side of the footlights. In Denver City, however, second-rate traveling companies were feted with the splendor usually reserved for visiting royalty. Inferior in culture and education to the East's smart theater set, the performers, nevertheless, were the picture of worldliness and sophistication to Denver theatergoers, many of whom were illiterate.

For all its avid pretense of literary and theatrical acumen, however, Denver City much preferred low comedy to high drama. "The people here want something more sensational than the elegant domestic or society drama," noted a newspaper article; "they require a certain amount of noise, or red light or *fanfare* to make them appreciate theatricals, and if they get this, with a liberal variety of plays, they will patronize more largely the drama in our city . . . . In addition to this, the things must be a little cheap."

252

Denver audiences would rather see on the stage, as they could, a live horse jump into a river and save the heroine than a heroic-size opera singer sing like a horse. The bizarre was infinitely more popular than the legitimate—the fat woman, the albino boy, freaks, and monsters drew heart-warming crowds.

But even if the sword-swallower outdrew the Shakespearean, the contortionist the contralto, the *News* continued to plug away in its demands for a legitimate theater, and eventually it got one, the Governor's Guard Hall at Fifteenth and Curtis; but business at the new hall was bad. The first season in particular was disastrous. Lavishly decorated with cages of canaries, paintings of the territorial governors, and—the *pièce de résistance*—an immense script of evergreen letters forming the words "A well regulated militia is the safety of a republic," the theater couldn't overcome a shallow stage, bad ventilation, and poor stage design which put the dressing rooms across the entrance hall from the stage. It is possible, too, that the fountain in front of the stage drowned out the performers.

The theater was first opened in February, 1873, then reopened the following November, and the *News*, which had long campaigned for the hall, gave a lamentable account of the performance: "Another attempt was made yesterday to open the theatre, but the success attending the effort amounted to nothing. A matinee was announced, but as there was nobody to see the play the house was not opened." That evening a lonely forty souls showed up, which so miffed the manager that he announced he was leaving. "With this," noted the *News*, "the audience turned toward the door, received their money, the gas was turned out, the house emptied, the actors went home, and the play was over, and probably the theatrical season in Denver."

The following year was little better, although Denver did turn out brilliantly to see the remarkably talented Mlle de Granville pick up a lager beer keg in her teeth. Unfortunately the management was unable to keep up such stunning performances, and the theater was sold, and sold again. Eventually it was purchased by Nate Forrester and renamed Forrester's Opera House, and al-

Flags flew, orchestras played, and all Denver turned out for the long-awaited opening of H. A. W. Tabor's Grand Opera House. Nearly as opulent as the theater, which Eugene Field called "modified Egyptian Moresque," was the opening night audience, which, whatever it was, was not "modified" (*Denver Public Library Western Collection*).

though its entertainments were not as toothsome as Mlle de Granville's, they were at least respectably prosperous.

By any other name the Tabor Grand Opera House would have been as splendid, although no title but "Tabor Grand," repetitious in a way, would have conjured up as quickly visions of the elegance

Whenever Baby Doe attended the theater, H. A. W. Tabor banked her
opera box with white lilies (*Denver Public Library Western Collection*).

and opulence of that fine house. As inveterate a showman as
Phineas T. Barnum himself (although P. T.'s flamboyance was
intentional and it is doubtful that Tabor's always was), H. A. W.
Tabor in a magnificent civic gesture presented the theater to
Denver in 1881.

The four-story, mansard-roofed (later squared up to form a
fifth story), brick and sandstone building, designed in Romanesque
style, set Tabor back $750,000 plus a few extra bills for sending
his architects and decorators to the Continent to cull the best in
design and furnishings from the opera houses of Europe. Eugene

255

Field called the architecture "modified Egyptian Moresque," and he described it as aptly as anyone, for the building combined touches of grand opera and music hall, from the Covent Garden Theatre in London and the Academy of Music in Paris to lesser houses of the eastern United States. The interior, which seated fifteen hundred, was finished in Japanese cherry with Italian marble pilasters, wainscotings, and lintels. From the cathedral glass dome in the beamed ceiling hung a huge gas-jet chandelier of cut crystal. The private boxes, which rose in tiers, were lined in heavy silk fabrics from Lyons that cost $150 a yard and were canopied with rare Italian tapestries. The first box was reserved for Tabor and identified with a plaque bearing his name wrought in silver from his Matchless mine. After Tabor and Baby Doe were married, Tabor banked his private box with white lilies whenever his wife attended a performance.

The famed curtain, hand painted by Robert Hopkin, a Detroit artist, was a bower of Roman ruins with beasts of prey lurking in the shadows of a crumbling temple and the lines of a poem:

> *So fleet the works of man*
> *Back to the earth again*
> *Ancient and holy things*
> *Fade like a dream*

In a strangely prescient gesture Tabor insisted that the last line of the stanza be omitted: "And the hand of the master is dust."

The public rooms were decorated with gilt mirrors, panel pictures of wild-flower designs, and a painting of Shakespeare, which looked down at theater patrons only briefly. A story that made the rounds of Denver society, no doubt originated by Eugene Field, who found Tabor's airs satirically funny, tells of an incident that supposedly took place on opening night when Tabor looked up at the painting and nudged manager Bill Bush. "Who's that up there?"

"Shakespeare."

"Who the hell is he?"

"Why, the greatest playwright who ever lived."

"Well, what has he ever done for Colorado! Take him down and put up my picture."

256

At its height, the opera house was a collection of Victorian extravagances. The curtain, hand painted, bore part of a strangely prophetic poem (*Denver Public Library Western Collection*).

Opening night was the gaudiest event in Denver history. Ladies turned out in décolleté gowns with ostrich plumes in their hair and the family jewels (which in Denver might be a full ten years old) slung around their necks. Augusta Tabor stayed at home while Baby Doe, who was soon to claim her husband, hid in the parquette section, heavily veiled. Even Tabor shunned the private box and stayed in the wings looking awkward and out of place. When he was called to the stage to be given an album autographed by everyone who had participated in building the theater and a gold watch and fob, purchased by Denver's leading citizens at five dollars a throw, he shuffled out in acute embarrassment and gave a muffled speech of acceptance. After Baby Doe's death, the watch and fob were found in a bundle of rags in the shack at the Matchless mine in Leadville that had been her squalid home for thirty years.

Emma Abbott and her English Grand Opera Company performed opening night, according to the silk programs, and later artists included Oscar Wilde (who merely shrugged when asked what he thought of the theater, the great Modjeska, Minnie Maddern (who performed again as Mrs. Fiske), John Drew, Lily Langtry, and Edwin Booth, who was so annoyed when the Tabor family arrived late, as it usually did to attract attention, that he stopped the performance, glared at the first box, and said in contempt that he would continue for those who had the taste to appreciate him.

Another Tabor Opera House performer was Sarah Bernhardt, who failed to inspire in all Denver theatergoers the adulation she created elsewhere. Eugene Field, in particular, was not impressed with her and wrote one of his famous one-line dramatic criticisms of her: "Last night in front of the Tabor Theatre there drew up an empty cab, from which Mme. Bernhardt alighted." Field delighted in baiting the performers, and one of his favorite tricks, pulled on Mrs. Fiske, was to throw a bouquet of flowers on the stage with a string attached to it. Every time the actress attempted to pick it up, Field moved it.

Like the rest of Tabor's empire, the splashy opera house operated a heady few years before being swallowed up by creditors. It began

Much loved by Denver theatergoers, the Broadway was a simple brown box whose outside gave little clue to the Meccan horrors within (*Denver Public Library Western Collection*).

going downhill about the time of World War I, when it became a cheap melodrama and vaudeville house, the upper rooms housing a series of seedy operations, including illegal gambling. Eventually the theater was turned into a second-run motion-picture house specializing in Westerns and Mexican movies. Every few years the management presented a notoriously inaccurate sentimental movie about the Tabors, showing the destitute former millionaire expiring in front of the theater. Like many other Denver landmarks, the Tabor Opera House was torn down a few years ago for no apparent reason, and the site at Sixteenth and Curtis now is the site of a Federal Reserve building.

Although the Broadway Theatre lacked the flamboyance of the Tabor Opera House, its opening night was nearly as spectacular. Society editors wrote columns of detailed descriptions of gowns and jewels and lists of who was "In the Boxes" or "In the Parquette." A thousand theatergoers crossed the 130–foot stretch of encaustic tile at the theater entrance and plunged into the East Indian bower that first night. With cries of delight they viewed the theater interior—a curtain showing an Indian street scene featuring a canopied elephant lumbering along. Groups of natives were pictured standing near a great wall "behind which tropical trees wave greeting to the audience." On either side of the great curtain, tiers of canopied boxes rose in Indian splendor while behind their screens of harem fretwork entwined with Indian-printed jute velour curtains, the box holders peeped at the audience. The olive green railings of the twenty-five boxes, "which a man that is addicted to color blindness might call old gold," matched the plush of the parquette chairs, thoughtfully placed in "variations of altitude calculated to bid defiance to Leghorn hats of generous brims, which ladies ofttimes wear to the horror of the unfortunate who sits behind them."

Behind the scenes the Broadway Theatre was every bit as elegant as it was in front of the curtain. A counterweight system operated the scenery, hydraulic cylinders the curtain. The twenty dressing rooms were the "embodiment of cleanliness" and larger than many "furnished rooms for rent." There were two star dressing rooms, and the Denver Victorians, impressed with such things, bragged that one of them contained the only theater dressing-room bathtub in the country.

Erected in 1890 by William H. Bush as a theater-hotel combination with the adjoining Metropole Hotel, the Broadway Theatre—its brick-box exterior as plain as the East Indian interior was opulent—was adored by generations of Denverites. Miss Emma Juch and her opera company, which brought along five railroad cars full of scenery (fortunately, since the theater backdrops had not yet arrived), performed *Carmen* on opening night, accompanied by a 150-voice chorus. The theater later presented the divine Sarah, and in one evening gave its audience a combination of a John L. Sullivan fight and a melodrama, *Honest Hearts and Willing Hands*.

In time the Broadway outranked the Tabor in theater productions and itself was outshone by the Denham, erected in 1913. Turned into a movie house, the Broadway never was subjected to the degradation that befell the Tabor, probably because its uptown location at Seventeenth and Broadway remained a good address. It still was a first-class theater when it was torn down in the 1950's to make way for the United Bank of Denver complex.

Long after Elitch Gardens was opened (at which time no one had an inkling it would ever be a first anything), that theater was discovered to be the oldest stock-company theater in the country, and the "oldest" brag was clapped onto its advertisements.

Built in 1890 in an apple orchard that had been turned into a garden area and zoo, Elitch's theater was designed for vaudeville and didn't present its first drama until several years after it opened. John Elitch, the proprietor, a restaurateur and theater manager, died the year after the gardens opened, but his wife Mary kept the theater going. Affectionately known as "The Lady of the Gardens," Mary Elitch, who had a shrewd eye for showmanship (she liked to make her rounds in a cart drawn by a trained ostrich) and acumen for business despite her curious refusal to serve liquor on the grounds, introduced drama to Elitch fans in the little cupola-topped vaudeville building that looked more like a fancy Eastern beach hotel than a legitimate theater.

261

The Tabor Opera House's decorator was a piker
compared to the man who built an Arabian

Nights temple inside the Broadway (*Denver Public Library Western Collection*).

Over the years Elitch's presented hundreds of actors in an assortment of plays. James O'Neill, father of playwright Eugene, was a leading man. Cecil B. De Mille played bit parts. Douglas Fairbanks, a Denver schoolboy, scrubbed the stage floor to earn a ticket to a Shakespearean play and returned a few years later to join the stock company. Mrs. Minnie Maddern Fiske played at Elitch's, and so did Sarah Bernhardt, appearing in her famous *La Dame aux Camélias* on one of her equally famous (and nearly as repetitious) farewell tours. Ecstatic about animals, the divine Sarah made the rounds of the zoo with Mrs. Elitch and fairly smothered a lion with affection. Fredric March was a member of the Elitch Stock Company, and so was Florence Eldridge until the two were married and the theater decided it wasn't romantic for a husband and wife to play opposite each other. Later Elitch performers who gained national fame were Grace Kelly, David Wayne, and Patricia Neal.

For the most part, Elitch's shows were light, family-style comedies, but in 1917 the theater put on a shockingly realistic play entitled *Salvation Nell*, a piece so wicked it had stunned even New York audiences when an actor audaciously uttered, "God damn!" The *Denver Post* called it horrible, and its reviewer said he'd sooner take his daughter on a pleasure tour of Market Street than let her see a performance of *Salvation Nell*.

Although most of Denver's theaters admittedly played down to their audiences, the Elitch Gardens Stock Company made an honest attempt to bring good drama to the city, all the more surprising because it was located in the heart of a colorful amusement park. Mary Elitch's innate showmanship, which caused her first to open a picnic area, zoo, and vaudeville theater (then change the vaudeville to a stock company) and to bring popular athletic and balloon acts to the park, eventually led her to install the tricky paraphernalia of a midway. Eventually the amusement park games and rides outdid the theater in attracting visitors. "Not to See Elitch's is Not to See Denver" was the cumbersome expostulation thrown at them, and strangely enough it worked. Thousands of visitors, along with hometowners, still flock to Elitch's just as Tom Thumb, Nat Good-

Elitch's theater building, erected in 1890, looked more like the flimsy pagoda of a midway than the home of the country's oldest stock company. Still standing, the original theater has been redecorated many times. The major remodeling took place in 1955 when quarters for the property department, a carpenter shop, and dressing rooms for the entire cast were added and the stage was enlarged; Elitch's reportedly has the only stage in the country big enough to fly a hundred-foot drop. During an earlier refurbishing, Mary Elitch hired a painter to touch up woodwork in the main dressing room, and he, to her horror, covered not only the trim but the door of the main dressing room, which had been autographed by all the famous stars who had played Elitch's.

win, and the invincible Phineas T. Barnum did seventy-five years ago to attend the opening of John and Mary Elitch's flower garden.

In a patriarchal era when woman's place was in the home, and rightly so, and any proper female quivered with fright at her

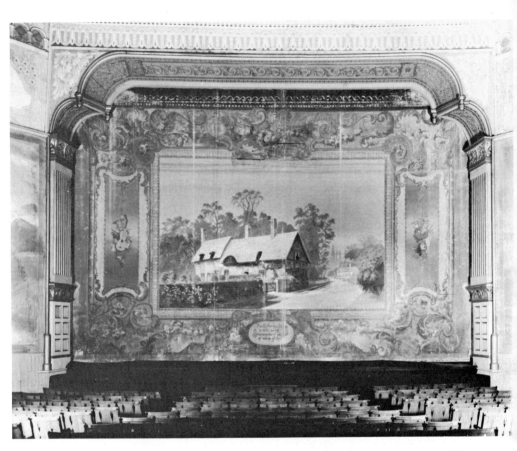

True to theatrical tradition, Elitch's featured a lavish curtain gaudily decorated, this one with a picture of Anne Hathaway's cottage and the inscription "Ann [*sic*] Hathaway's Cottage a mile away, / Shakespeare sought at close of day" (*Denver Public Library Western Collection*).

husband's condemnation if she so much as threatened conjugal bliss by doubting it, a man's place was in his club, be it BPOE, lodge, or literary group. Here he was safe from feminine impingement; here he might discuss politics surrounded by the air of good coronas or drink brandy free from the interference of women and children. A boy became a man when he joined a club; he shed childhood

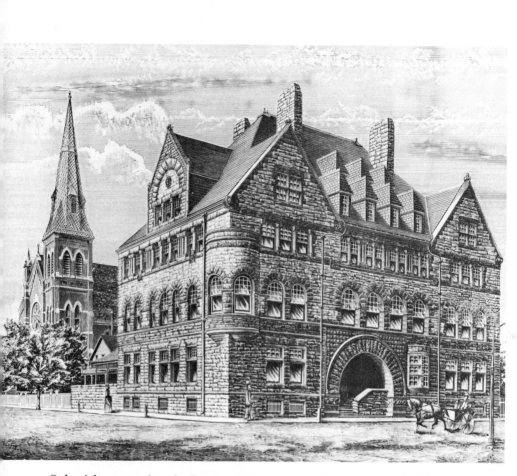

Only eight years after the Denver Club was formed, members were able to dip into the till and build this Cherry Creek Romanesque clubhouse. Located at the corner of Seventeenth and Glenarm, the Denver Club was a bastion of male dominion whose members liked to gather at the window whenever Maggie Brown appeared, dressed from head to toe in outlandish furs, poling her way down Seventeenth Street with her crook-like cane, and wag: "There goes Colorado's unique fur-bearing animal" (*Denver Public Library Western Collection*).

when he took the vows of a clubman, whether the mystic ritual of a Masonic order or the social conventions of a gentleman's club.

Lest for a moment one should think that because wives were excluded the club was some sort of raucous den, far from it. The club was subjected to as rigid a set of standards as the home and was equally sacrosanct. With its massive oak furniture, stuffed animal heads, and stuffy air, a club, although rigidly masculine, might also be incurably dull; but woe to the member who attempted to add spark by bringing a woman, proper or otherwise, through its formidable doors. A gentleman might take a female companion to a gambling club, to a discreet restaurant, or even to a hotel, but only a fool would attempt to bring her into the sacred confines of his club. When William H. Bryant, president of the Denver Club, brought two soiled doves into the men's taproom in defiance of house rules, so horrible a breach of etiquette had he made that the next morning club members found the following notice posted:

For violating the rules and for conduct unbecoming a gentleman William H. Bryant is denied privileges of the Denver Club for 30 days.

WILLIAM H. BRYANT, President

Gambling was frowned on in most clubs, except those devoted exclusively to games of chance, of course; and in the Denver Club, first in the pecking order of exclusively male fellowships, house rules forbade poker and other well-known gambling games, permitting only whist, hearts, and "Penny Boston" with a twenty-five-cent limit. The bylaws included, as well, a rule that personal checks in excess of twenty-five dollars could not be cashed by members.

Although their purposes were avowedly social, the clubs had also a practical business purpose. Political alliances were made by members lounging in comfortable oak chairs, and business deals were consummated over starched white tablecloths. With David H. Moffat, Nathaniel P. Hill, Walter S. Cheesman, the brothers Wolcott, James Duff, George W. Clayton, Moses Hallett, and Governor John L. Routt as members of the same club, business and politics were inevitable.

Fittingly enough, it was allowing females into the precincts

268

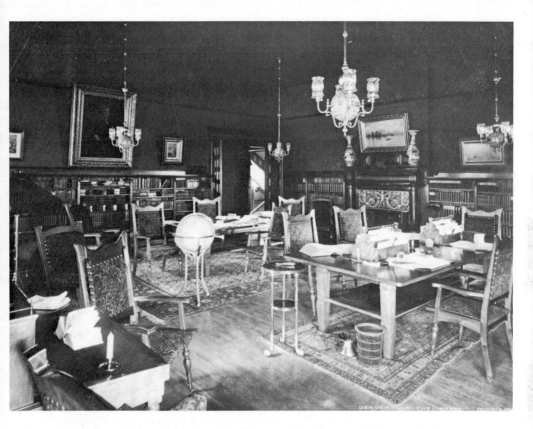

Placed for easy access in the stuffy library of the Denver Club were both
wastebasket and spittoon (*Denver Public Library Western Collection*).

hitherto consecrated to men, an idea perpetrated by the same
formidable movement that gave women the vote, that ended the
exclusiveness of the men's club, for—although it seldom was ad-
mitted—the club's real purpose was to provide a haven from
women. With the coming of femininity, pale table coverings and gilt
chairs began to replace the starched white cloths and oak great
chairs, cuspidors disappeared from parlors, and stuffed animal
heads were relegated to the basement; the clubs began to take
on the appearance of that social upstart the country club. And

when twittering females revealingly attired in long-john bathing suits invaded the swimming pools where only moments before splendid masculinity romped without so much as the decorum of a fig leaf, the days of male dominion were, indeed, a part of history.

There was little doubt that Denver's most formidable club was the hallowed Denver Club, where members would gather "evening after evening, talk, read, play billiards and smoke," and be "devoutly thankful that they are members of the club." Although none of the Denver Club card-carriers would have put it so succinctly, they would admit privately that, in the main, the writer was correct; they were, thank God, quite good enough to be extended membership.

Incorporated in 1880 by twenty-two of the city's august citizens, the Denver Club was the Western contemporary of Boston's Somerset Club or New York City's Union. Its members—according to Lee Casey, memorable *Rocky Mountain News* columnist—"made money, inherited money or married money. A few achieved all three." There was no question that its constituency was wealthy, for by 1880 it was able to build a massive rock clubhouse, portly and solid as the members themselves. Located at Seventeenth and Glenarm, the Denver Club Building was designed in Cherry Creek Romanesque style, hewn sandstone and granite, with Romanesque arches and a steep-pitched gabled roof. Inside was a healthy preponderance of oak furniture, cherry, oak, mahogany, walnut, and butternut paneling, fireplaces, and shiny cuspidors. Each bedroom had a fireplace and a brass bed. There were four porcelain tubs and one copper shower, and all the silverware was from Tiffany's. In the barbershop were individual shaving mugs for the members— Maxcy Tabor's, for instance, or Dennis Sullivan's with bright violets on the side. A specially built cellar under the Seventeenth Street sidewalk contained a $15,000 stock of wines. The pride of the Denver Club—and its symbol to those rejected for membership—was a stuffed moose head, shot by David Moffat, hung in the lobby.

After opening with a brilliant ball, the members, whom Richard

Built in the 1890's, the DAC looks on the outside much as it did seventy-five years ago. A fire in 1951 ruined a good part of the interior.

Harding Davis called "that most delightful coterie at the Denver Club which never sleeps," settled down to years of business and political intrigue. From the beginning, wrote a contemporary, "the club has been eminently successful though of so exclusive a nature that little of its workings has been known to outsiders."

Much of that exclusiveness, along with the aura of masculinity, had long since evaporated when the Denver Club sanctuary was torn down in 1953 and replaced by a modern office building whose top floors were made into a contemporary clubhouse. The old building itself had become an anachronism by the mid–1900's— nobody drank wine anymore, and Gillette Blue Blades in the bathroom at home had taken the place of a luxurious shave at the club with a straight razor and lather from a violet-decorated mug. And not only were members allowed to bring women into the taproom, but the girls could trundle in by themselves.

In an era when foot racers were national idols, when a gentleman prided himself as much on the cut of his figure as on the cut of a deck, it was natural that athletic clubs attracted a vast membership. The Denver Athletic Club was formed in 1884 when William R. Rathvon invited several gymnasts to join him in forming a sporting fraternity. Early meetings of the athletes were held in Liebhardt's fruit and grocery store on Holladay; then the club rented the Baptist church at Eighteenth and Curtis and maintained as well an athletic park on the site of East Denver High School. Their Romanesque clubhouse, located at 1325 Glenarm, was built in 1890 with funds raised through a membership drive. One hundred forty new members donned the DAC Raccoons' cherry and black uniforms at a lifetime membership fee of three hundred dollars each, exactly one hundred times the original initiation fee, a stiff lesson for laggards who had turned down Rathvon's three-dollar invitations just six years earlier.

Like most of Colorado's early clubs, the DAC today bears little resemblance to the early organization. Although the club still maintains a swimming pool and a complete gymnasium, its members are not always the sports of yesteryear. The only calisthenics some of them do is lifting cup to lip at the DAC's well-appointed bar.

DAC members were not above a little frivolity, all for a good cause, of course (*Denver Public Library Western Collection*).

Their gold pans were empty and their bellies were, too, but that didn't stop the Cherry Creek prospectors of 1858 from kneeling at their Victorian mecca, the Masonic lodge. Barely had they unpacked their gold-panning gear than half a dozen of the faithful gathered in a log cabin for ritualistic preparations. The All-Seeing Eye had sought them out even in the sands of the Cherry Creek. They formed a lodge, falseheartedly abandoned it when the entire

273

This sandstone imp still makes faces at passers-by on Welton. He's part of the Masonic Building, Sixteenth and Tremont.

274

membership rushed to the Gregory Diggings in search of gold, then took up the organization at the new location. In the meantime, less faithless souls had organized a cell in Auraria that eventually built a sandstone temple as embellished with symbols as the Masonic rites themselves.

Six stories of decorated Romanesque styling, the temple, at Sixteenth and Welton, was a complex of architectural fantasy—the façade was a collection of parapets, round turrets, pierced balustrades, bays, piers, dentilated string courses, richly carved capitals, enriched label moldings, gables, tympanums, foliated carving, molded and dress reveals, and loggias, the Welton Street entrance being a semi-circular arch encompassing entwined sandstone leaves and vines and cavorting imps and gargoyles.

The interior of the temple was as architecturally ornate as the exterior. The fourth floor, for instance, housed the Masonic rooms with the necessary preparation rooms, anterooms, organ loft, and grand reception room. Described in elaborate detail in an early newspaper account, the entrance to one room was a "curtained portiere of tasteful and elaborate design, the sides and upper portions being filled with intricate wrought iron grille work, studded with colored glass and supported by a frame work of richly carved and moulded woodwork." As colorful as the Masonic ceremony, the building nevertheless was no gaudier when built in 1890 than the average Denver office block. Today, its style spoiled by bricked-up windows, the Masonic building peers down at Sixteenth Street with sightless eyes.

EPILOGUE

THERE WAS A SENSE OF IRREVERENCE about Denver, Colorado, a flagrant disregard for the ambling beauty of the South Platte and the trickle of the Cherry Creek. With haste unencumbered by aesthetic restraint the early prospectors plunged over the banks brandishing their pie-shaped gold pans, ripped up the sands of the creek bed that had lain undisturbed for some large portion of an eternity, and threw up shacks along the meandering stream.

With the same sense of urgency they tore down the shacks and replaced them with unstable frame buildings that in turn gave way to brick ones. The same cycle of life and untimely death continued; it still goes on. The sense of irreverence lingers.

Stand to watch a fine old mansion come down. Watch its linen-fold carving, its polished brass, its delicate-hued stained glass ripped out as some hunter would disembowel his kill. In its place a thin-skinned apartment goes up, its façade the look of a piece of wrapping paper with stairways trailing up its sides like fire escapes.

277

Some sensibly commercial soul, some just-folks, comfortable-as-an-old-shoe kind of guy will wander by and mutter amiably, "Yup, that's progress."

Progress, we are told by the land hawkers, the promoters, the Chamber of Commerce backslappers, is unequivocally new. It is contemporary. It is current. Progress is a flat-chested brick box that replaces a granite castle. Progress is a blacktop parking area that covers the site of Charpiot's. Progress is a filling station. Progress is a vacant lot.

Noticeable because it is untouched by the architectural pillaging going on around it, is Larimer Square, a block-long restoration of Larimer Street. Conceived by a Denver woman with a belief that Colorado history was getting a raw deal, the idea for Larimer Square was more than for simple preservation. Larimer Square, designed as a profit-making venture grounded on a corporate structure with substantial capital, is an integration of shops, restaurants, galleries, and night spots remarkably restored to depict early Denver. It is, if you take your history in firsts, Denver's most historic block. Architecturally, it is among the city's most diverse and most representational blocks. It is an impressive example of responsible heritage.

It is paradoxical that the tenements of would-be Bavarian style that are usurping the mansions of the past, whose catastrophic designs have the undeniable look of orange crates, must regress to the era of their elders for architectural interest. In front of Brooks Towers—a hulking pillar covered with iron-foundry tracery that punctures the skyline of lower downtown Denver, a blatant cacophony that squats on the gravesite of the Mining Exchange Building—stands the glorious statue of the Colorado miner that once adorned Brooks Towers' predecessor. One fervently hopes that he will swing his pick at his captives who have toppled him from his perch in the sky and chained him to a concrete cliff in front of that air-conditioned cage.

Even passionate historians and architectural conservationists are reluctant to salvage all of Denver's past. A static city is a stagnant one. Such architectural horrors as the Railroad Exchange

278

Building would have been better left unbuilt. But Denver needs a respect for its past, a sense of time and timelessness that is lacking even among the city's major planners.

An urban renewal project, passed in 1967, will do to the city's architectural heritage what independent promoters haven't quite accomplished in half a century. With a total disregard for the past, the project is wiping out blocks of Denver's most distinctive buildings, many pictured in this book. Its one crumb tossed to historians is retention of the Daniels & Fisher tower, a landmark to be sure, but one built well into the twentieth century. The gentle iron columns and peach-color tile of the older part of the building, the handsome Barclay Block, the row of once-lavish gambling halls at Sixteenth and Larimer, all are going before the bulldozer of "progress."

There is no need for it. The waste is senseless. There is still time to salvage Denver's distinctive look, to preserve this dimension for Denver's future. No one asks that everything be saved, just a few pieces, a building here and there to give a sense of continuity to Larimer and Market streets, a few façades to add light and shadow and architectural interest to Lawrence. There is so little left.

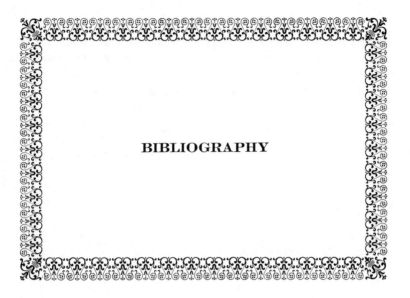

BIBLIOGRAPHY

NEWSPAPERS AND MAGAZINES

Colorado Catholic
Colorado Magazine
Daily News (Denver)
Denver Catholic Register
Denver Post
Denver Republican
Denver Times
Denver Tribune
Harper's Weekly
Frank Leslie's Illustrated Weekly
Mountain & Plain History Notes
The Review (Denver Public Schools)
Rocky Mountain News
The Trail
University of Denver Clarion
University of Denver Magazine
Western Architect and Building News

BOOKS AND PAMPHLETS

Adair, Cornelia. *My Diary*. Austin, University of Texas Press, 1965.

Architecture of Denver Hotels. Denver, Writers Program, Colorado, 1941.

Arps, Louisa Ward. *Denver in Slices*. Denver, Sage Books, 1959.

Art Work of Denver, Colorado. Denver, Gravure Illustration, 1902.

Bancroft, Caroline. *Silver Queen*. Boulder, Johnson, 1959.

———. *Six Racy Madams of Colorado*. Boulder, Johnson, 1965.

Barney, Libeus. *Letters of the Pike's Peak Gold Rush*. San Jose, Talisman, 1959.

Beebe, Lucius. *The Big Spenders*. Garden City, Doubleday, 1966.

Buildings and Historic Sites of Denver. Denver, Writers Program, Colorado, c. 1940.

Byers, William N., and Jno. H. Kellom. *Hand Book to the Gold Fields*. Chicago, D. B. Cook & Co., 1859.

Casey, Sister M. Celestine, and Sister M. Edmond Fern. *Loretto in the Rockies*. Denver, 1943.

Denver Red Book. Denver, 1892.

Distinctive Denver. Denver, Chamber of Commerce, 1924.

Dunham, Harold H., ed. *The Brand Book*. Denver, University of Denver Press, 1951.

Fowler, Gene. *Timber Line*. New York, Blue Ribbon, 1933.

Hill, Alice Polk. *Colorado Pioneers in Picture and Story*. Denver, Brock-Haffner, 1915.

Hill, Emma Shepard. *The Central Presbyterian Church*. Denver, Eames, 1930.

Karshner, David. *Silver Dollar*. New York, Crown, 1932.

Life in Denver. Denver, Writers Program, Colorado, 1941.

Mazzulla, Fred and Jo. *Brass Checks and Red Lights*. Denver, 1966.

Meline, James F. *Two Thousand Miles on Horseback*. New York, Hurd & Houghton, 1867.

Miller, Max. *Holladay Street*. New York, Signet, 1962.

Mumey, Nolie. *History of the Early Settlements of Denver (1599–1860)*. Glendale, Arthur H. Clark, 1942.

Niehaus, Fred Raymond. *70 Years of Progress: History of Banking in Colorado, 1876–1946*. Washington, Federal Deposit Insurance Corp., 1948.

Otis, James. *Seth of Colorado*. New York, American Book Company, 1912.

Parkhill, Forbes. *The Wildest of the West*. Denver, Sage Books, 1951.

Perkin, Robert L. *The First Hundred Years: An Informal History of Denver and the* Rocky Mountain News. Garden City, Doubleday, 1959.

Richardson, Albert D. *Beyond the Mississippi*. Hartford, American Publishing Company, 1867.

Scamehorn, G. N. *Behind the Scenes or Denver by Gaslight*. Denver, George A. Shirley, 1894.

Schoberlin, Melvin. *From Candles to Footlights*. Denver, Old West, 1941.

Smiley, Jerome C. *History of Denver*. Denver, Denver Times, 1901.

———. *Semi-Centennial History of the State of Colorado*. Chicago, Lewis, 1913.

Thayer, William M. *Marvels of the New West*. Norwich, Henry Bill, 1887.

Vickers, W. B. *History of the City of Denver*. Chicago, O. L. Baskin, 1880.

Wharton, J. E. *History of the City of Denver*. Denver, Byers & Dailey, 1866.

White, James H. *The First Hundred Years of Central Presbyterian Church*. Denver, Great Western Stockman, 1960.

Willison, George F. *Here They Dug the Gold*. New York, Reynal & Hitchcock, 1946.

Wyer, Malcolm Glenn, ed. *The Lookout*. Denver, Denver Public Library, 1928.

Zamonski, Stanley, and Teddy Keller. *The Fifty-niners*. Denver, Sage Books, 1961.

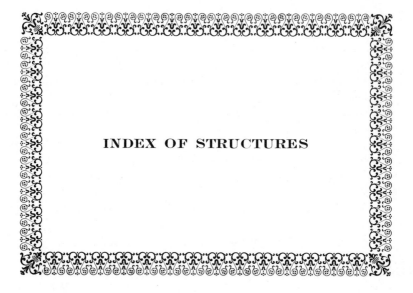

INDEX OF STRUCTURES

Albany Hotel: 90
Alvord House: 89
American House: 17, 84
Ankers Emporium of Fashion: 160
Apollo Hall: 246
Arcade Gambling Hall: 217

Bailey, J. W., home: 64
Barclay Block: 134
Basset, Amy, house of prostitution: 243
Batione Hotel: 232
Baur's Restaurant: 112
Birks Cornforth grocery store: 123
Birnard, Belle, house of prostitution: 233
Boettcher, Claude K., home: *see* Chees-man, Walter, home
Bonfils, Frederick, home: 71
Boston Building: 147, 148
Brinker Collegiate Institute and Com-mercial College: 224
Broadway Theatre: 259, 262–63
Broadwell House: 78, 249

Brown, Mrs. J. J., home (House of Lions): 65, 66
Brown Palace Hotel: 100, 102, 103, 104
Buchtel Memorial Chapel: 181
Buildings, miscellaneous: homes, 26, 28, 34, 36, 45, 46, 47, 50, 72, 73; apart-ments, 49, 75, 76; stores, 122, 125, 129, 130, 132; cribs, 231

C. A. Cook & Company Banking House: 158, 159
Carnegie Hall: 183
Cast-iron fencing: 37
Central Presbyterian Church: 172, 174
Chamberlain Observatory: 182
Chamberlain's Ambrotype & Photogra-phic Gallery: 246
Charpiot's Hotel and Restaurant: *see* Charpiot's Restaurant
Charpiot's Restaurant: 108
Chase, Ed, home: 51
Cheesman, Walter, drugstore: 159, 160
Cheesman, Walter, home: 60

Cheesman Building: 135
Cheney's Billiard Hall: 159, 197
Chever, Charles, home: 31
Chever Block: 142
Chicken Coop: 219
"Church of the Seven Spot of Dia-
monds": see Central Presbyterian
Church
City Bakery: 201, 205
City Hall: 149
Clark, Gruber & Co.: 155
Colorado Bakery: 120
Colorado Mining Stock Exchange Build-
ing: 138, 139, 140
Colorado National Bank: 160; see also
Cheesman, Walter, drugstore
Conservative Baptist Theological Semi-
nary: see Bonfils, Frederick, home
Cook & Company Banking House: see
C. A. Cook & Company Banking
House
Corona Street School: 190
Criterion Saloon: 195
Croke, Thomas B., home: 58
Curtis-Clark Building: 128
Customs House: see Federal Building

Daniels, Fisher & Co.: 151, 152, 153, 154
Daniels, William B., home: 32, 221, 222,
223
Daniels & Brown: 197
Denver: overview of, 19, 54
Denver and Rio Grande Railway: 136
Denver Athletic Club: 271
Denver City Railway Company power-
house: 141
Denver Club: 267, 269
Denver House: 193
Denver Theatre: 249
D. G. Peabody, clothing store: 204
Dora Moore School: see Corona Street
School

Eldorado Hotel: 13
Elephant Corral: 197; site of, 198
Elitch Gardens: 265, 266
Elitch's Palace: see Tortoni's Restaurant
Emanuel Episcopalian Church: 171
Evans, John, home: 39
Evans, William Gray, home: 40
Evans Chapel: 167
Equitable Building: 146, 147

Exchange Bank: see Chever Block

Farmer, Joseph P., home: 42–43
Federal Building: 150
Field, Eugene, home: 27
Fillmore Block: 204
First German Methodist Episcopal
Church: 168
First National Bank: 156, 157, 159, 160
Fisher, William Garret, home: 55

Gazette Printing Office: 197
Governor's mansion: see Grant, Gover-
nor James B., governor's mansion;
Cheesman, Walter, home
Grand Central Hotel: 92; see also Mark-
ham Hotel
Grant, Governor James B., governor's
mansion: 59
Gumry Hotel, debris of: 96
G. W. Kassler & Co.: 197

Hendrie, Edwin B., home: see Richtho-
fen, Baron Walter von, home
Hense & Gottesleben: see J. H. Hense &
P. Gottesleben
Heywood & Co.: 204
H. H. Tammen Curio Company: 150
Hill, Mrs. Crawford, home: 67
Hill, Nathaniel P., home: 41
Hindry, John B., home: 33
Hirschberg, R. L., cigars and tobacco:
108
Holladay Overland Mail & Express Co.:
16
Horner, J. W., home: 30
House of Lions: see Brown, Mrs. J. J.,
home
House of Mirrors: see Rogers, Jennie,
House of Mirrors
Humphreys, A. E., home: see Grant,
Governor James B., governor's man-
sion

Iliff, J. S., home: 38
Iliff School: 180
L'Imperiale Hotel: 95
Inter-Ocean Club: 121, 122, 123
Inter-Ocean Hotel: 86
Iron Building: 143

Jackson, William H., photographic
studio: 126, 127, 217

285

J. G. Vawter & Co.: 17
J. H. Hense & P. Gottesleben: 108, 151

Kassler & Co.: *see* G. W. Kassler & Co.
Kavanagh Vidal & Co.: 110
Kinneavy Terrace: 74
Kountze Brothers Bank: *see* Colorado National Bank
Kramer, George W., home: 48

Lange & Hance: 207
Larimer, General William H., cabin: 11
Lawrence Street Methodist Church: 163, 164
LeFevre, Judge Owen, home: 61
Lindner Building: *see* Mapelli-Lindner-Sigman buildings
Londoner, Wolfe, home: 29
Londoner Building: 144
Loretto Heights College: 180, 185

"Main Hall": *see* Regis College
Manhattan Restaurant: 113, 217
Mapelli-Lindner-Sigman buildings: 131
Markham Hotel: 93; *see also* Grand Central Hotel
Masonic Building: 274
May-D&F: *see* Daniels, Fisher & Co.
Miller's Boston Boot and Shoe Store: 151
Moffat, David H., home: 44
Mozart Billiard Hall: *see* Criterion Saloon
Murphy's Exchange: 217

Nassau Block: *see* Tabor Block

Occidental Billiard Hall: 197, 201
"Old Main": *see* University Hall
Overland Despatch: 159

Pacific House: *see* Broadwell House
Palace Theatre: 197, 207
Patterson, Senator Thomas, home: *see* Croke, Thomas B., home
Peabody, clothing store: *see* D. G. Peabody, clothing store
Pell, George, tombstone: 117
Pell's Oyster House: 116
Pioneer Building: 137
Planter's House: 79
Postal Telegraph Company office: *see* Chever Block

Progressive Club: 200

Railroad Building: 137
Regis College: 187
Richthofen, Baron Walter von, home: 62
Rocky Mountain News, offices: 12, 14, 15
Rogers, Jennie, House of Mirrors: 235; *see also* Silks, Mattie
Russell-Smith cabin (first building on Cherry Creek): 11

St. Cajetan's Roman Catholic Church: 177
St. John's Church in the Wilderness: 169, 170
St. Mary's Roman Catholic Church: 176
Salvation Army building: *see* Lawrence Street Methodist Church
Sayre, Hal, home: 57
Sheedy, Dennis, home: 56
Silks, Mattie, house of prostitution: 238; *see also* Rogers, Jennie, House of Mirrors
"Slaughterhouse": *see* Murphy's Exchange
Stoiber, Lena, home: 68, 69
Stoiberhof: *see* Stoiber, Lena, home

Tabor, H. A. W., home: 63; *see also* Bailey, J. W., home
Tabor Block: 133
Tabor Grand Opera House: 254, 255, 257
Tammen, Harry Heye, home: 70
Tammen Curio Company: *see* H. H. Tammen Curio Company
Tappan Building: 120
Temple Emanuel: 178
Tivoli Beer Hall: 207
Tortoni's Restaurant: 110
Tremont House (antique shop): 35
Tremont House (hotel): 82
Trinity Methodist Church: 165, 166

University Hall ("Old Main"): 180

Vawter & Co.: *see* J. G. Vawter & Co.
Venetian bell tower: 153
Victory Hotel: *see* Alvord House

286

Wells, Fargo & Co., offices: 16, 120, 121;
see also Holladay Overland Mail &
Express Co.
Wentworth Hotel: 87

West Lindell Hotel: 81
Windsor Hotel: 97, 98, 99
Wolfe Hall: 188, 189
Wootton Block: 12

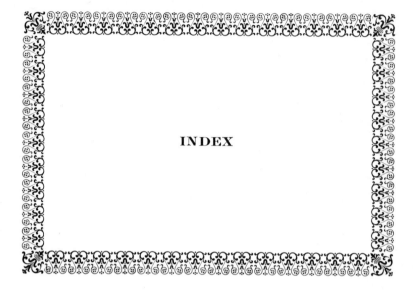

INDEX

Abbott, Emma: 258
Adams, Charles: 96
Adriance, Rev. Jacob: 163
After the Bath (picture): 220
Alexis (Russian grand duke): 77, 83, 105, 109
Argo, Colo.: 27, 41
Auraria, Colo.: 4, 6, 8, 14, 25, 191
Austin, Robert A.: 216

Bailey, J. W.: 64
Baldwin, Lucky: 241
Baldwin, Verona: 241–42
Ballard, Judge: 215
Barbour, Frances Minerva: *see* Chase, Mrs. Ed (third wife)
Barker, A. H.: 4
Barney, Libeus: 8–10, 245, 248
Barnum, Colo.: 27
Barnum, Phineas T.: 182, 251, 255, 265
Baron di Gallotti (Don Carlos): 206
Baroness di Gallotti (Stephanie): 206
Basset, Amy: 242

Batione, Mrs. C. I.: 232
Battle of Glorieta Pass: 162
Baur, Mrs. O. P.: 112
Baur, O. P.: 87, 111–12
Beck, John: 162
Beebe, Lucius: 65
Behind the Scenes or Denver By Gaslight (book): 215
Belford, James B.: 88
Belmont, Nellie: 204
Bent, Sadie: 203
Berkey, John: 133
Bernhardt, Sarah: 258, 261, 264
Binford, E. J.: 94
Birnard, Belle: 233, 239, 240
Blake, Charles H.: 5–6
Bliss, L. W.: 79–80
Blue Row: 229
Boettcher, Claude K.: 60
Bonfils, Frederick: 58, 71
Booth, Edwin: 258
Bowen, Tom: 208
Boyce, Barney: 216

288

Brinker, Joseph: 217, 224
Broadwell, J. M.: 78
Brown, Blanche: 239, 241
Brown, George W.: 8
Brown, Henry C.: 50, 52, 78, 101, 103
Brown, Margaret Tobin (Mrs. J. J.): 27, 52, 65–69, 267
Brown, Samuel: 8
Brown's Bluff: 50, 52
Bryan, William Jennings: 89, 102, 183
Bryant, William H.: 268
Buchtel, Henry Augustus: 181–83, 186
Bucking the Tiger (picture): 220, 225
Buffalo Bill: *see* Cody, William F.
Bush, William: 256, 261
Byers, William N.: 6, 14, 40, 58, 85, 198–99, 215 225, 252

Campion, John: 52
Capitol Hill: 24, 45, 52, 55–60, 64, 67
Carty, Mother Praxedes: 186
Casey, Lee: 270
Casey, Pat: 250–51
Chaffee, Jerome B.: 156
Chaffee Light Artillery: 149
Charpiot, Fred: 105, 107–108
Chase, Ed: 51, 200, 202–204, 208–14, 216, 218, 220–23, 225
Chase, Mrs. Ed: first Mrs. Chase, 204; second Mrs. Chase, 205; third Mrs. Chase, 51, 205, 208
Chase, John: 202
Cheesman, Walter: 60, 159, 268
Cherry Creek: 3–4, 6, 8, 13–15, 17, 27, 39, 41, 111, 114, 191, 273, 277
Cherry Creek Diggings: 7
Chever, Charles: 31, 142
Chivington, Colonel John M.: 161–62, 202
Chucovich, Vaso: 213, 216, 218, 220–21, 224
Church, William: 52
Clark, Austin M.: 8
Clark, Milton E.: 8
Clarke, Clarence J.: 128
Clay, Cassius: 252
Clayton, George W.: 201, 268
Clow (killed in Murphy's Exchange): 214
Cody, William F. (Buffalo Bill): 77, 83, 87, 89, 96, 98–99, 105
Colorado Cavalry: 202

Colorado Seminary: *see* University of Denver
Colorado Volunteers: 162, 250
Cornforth, Birks: 123
Croke, Thomas B.: 52, 58
Currigan, Martin: 149
Curtis, Rodney: 128
Custer, General George A.: 83
Cutler, Benjamin O.: 85

Daniels, Mrs. William B.: 216
Daniels, William B.: 32, 216, 221
Davis, Richard Harding: 270–71
Davis, Walter Juan: 89
Deadeye Dick: 213
de Camp, Leona: 240
de Granville, Mlle: 253–54
De Mille, Cecil B.: 264
Denver, James W.: 91
Derring, Belle: 203
Devere, Bill: 210
Doe, Harvey: 241
Dougherty, Mike: 247–48, 250–51
Drew, John: 258
Duff, James: 268
Dunraven, Lord: 105
Dupuy, Louis: 115
Dyer, Father John: 164

Eckart, John M.: 133
Eldridge, Florence: 264
Elitch, John: 88, 108, 111, 261, 265
Elitch, Mary: 261, 264–65
Elitch Gardens Stock Co.: 264
English Grand Opera Co.: 258
Estes, A. H.: 88
Evans, John: 4, 18, 24, 27, 39, 40, 81, 137, 167, 179
Evans, Josephine: 167
Evans, William Gray: 40

Fairbanks, Douglas: 264
Farmer, Joseph P.: 42
Field, Cyrus W.: 85
Field, Eugene: 27, 106, 144, 209, 254–56, 258
Fisher, George: 162
Fisher, William Garret: 55
Fiske, Minnie Maddern: 258, 264
Forrester, Nate: 253
Forsyth, Major George A.: 83
Fowler, Gene: 240–41, 243

Foy, Eddie: 208
French, Mme: 203
Fries, Leeah J.: *see* Rogers, Jennie

Gage, David A.: 88
Garden, Mary: 101
Gates, "Bet-A-Million": 209
Gilpin, Governor William: 81, 250
Glenmore, Zell: 203
Globeville, Colo.: 27
Goldrick, Owen J.: 8, 251
Goode, William H.: 163
Goodwin, Nat: 264
Grant, Governor James B.: 59
Greeley, Horace: 7, 9, 194
Gregory Diggings: 275
Gregory Gulch: 247
Gruber, E. Henry: 8
Gumry, Peter: 95

Hague, Lord: 107-108
Hall, Minnie A.: 239, 242
Hallett, Moses: 268
Hamilton, Eva: 203
Harrison, Charley: 195–99
Hart, Dean Henry Martyn: 209
Haydee, Rose: 246–48
Haydee's Star Co.: 247
Heatley, Francis P.: 200, 210
Held, Anna: 102
Hendrie, Edwin B.: 62
Highlands (Denver suburb): 25, 228
Hill, Mrs. Crawford: 41, 65, 67
Hill, Nathaniel P.: 41, 268
Hindry, John B.: 33
Hoffses, Al: 216
Holladay, Ben: 16
Holmes, Jennie: 239
Hopkin, Robert: 256
Howe, Herbert A.: 182
Hughes, John J.: 213
Humphreys, A. E.: 59
Hunt, Helen: 85
Hutchins, Roswell: 4

Iliff, J. W.: 180
Indian Row: 228

Jackson, William H.: 93, 126–27, 217
Jacob, John Joseph: 112
Juch, Emma: 261
Jump, Ed: 197

Kelly, Etta: 235
Kelly, Grace: 264
Kerr, James P.: 214–15
King, G. W.: 80
Kingston, John: 228
Koch, Fred: 219
Kountze, Harold B.: 52, 160
Kramer, George W.: 48

Lady of the Gardens: *see* Elitch, Mary
Lamon, Ward Hill: 88
LaMont, Ada: 227–28
Lamy, Bishop Jean Baptiste: 162
Langrishe, John S.: 247–48, 250–51
Langtry, Lily: 258
Larimer, General William H.: 4, 11, 21, 173
Larimer, William H. H. (General Larimer's son): 5
Lauder, Harry: 102
Leavenworth Party: 5
LeFevre, Eva French: 61
LeFevre, Judge Owen: 61
Lewis, Eva: 240
Little Egypt (picture): 220
Logan, Jennie: 203
London, Belle: 241
Londoner, Wolfe: 29, 144
Lorelei, The (picture): 220
Loretto, Sisters of: 184–86
Loretto Heights Academy: *see* Loretto Heights College
Loretto Heights College: 180, 184–86
Lovejoy, Rose: 241
Lovell, Lillis: 241
Lovell, Lois: 241

McCook, E. M.: 83
McCook, Mrs. E. M.: 83
McHatton (Denver coroner): 230
Machebeuf, Bishop Joseph P.: 161–62, 175–76
McLean, Evelyn Walsh: 102
March, Fredric: 264
Markham, V. D.: 91
Marsh, Emma: 203
Marshall, Tom: 90
Marshall (in fight at Murphy's Exchange): 214
Masterson, Bat: 90, 195, 210, 213
Meeker, Mrs. Nathan: 96
Meier, Theodore L.: 112

Ming, John: 7
Modjeska (actress): 258
Moffatt, David H.: 44, 52, 156, 268, 270
Montclair (Denver suburb): 27, 62
Moon, Jim: 212–13
Moore, Effie: 210
Morning (picture): 220
Mosconi, Dave: 116
Mosconi, Louis: 116
Murat, Katrina: 7, 78
Murat, Count Henri: 7, 78, 194, 201

Neal, Patricia: 264
Nichols, Charles: 4
Night (picture): 220

Ogilvy, Lord: 111
O'Neill, Eugene: 264
O'Neill, James: 264
Ouray (Ute chief): 105

Pahaska: *see* Cody, William F.
Parlor Match, The (picture): 220
Pat Casey's Night Hands (play): 250
Patterson, Thomas M.: 58, 91
Pearce, Richard B.: 52
Pell, George: 117–18
Perry, Mme: 203
Pickle, John: 80
Pierson, Charles O.: 213
Pinhorn, Richard: 114
Pioneer Ladies Aid Society: 7
Plezes, Rev.: 173
Pollock, Tom: 6
Preston, Lizzie: 203, 240

Quality Hill: 52, 190
Quayle, William: 236

Ramage, J. D.: 6
Rathvon, William R.: 272
Raverdy, John B.: 175
Red Book: 239
Regis College: 187
Rhoda, Mme: 203
Richardson, Albert Dean: 9, 246
Richthofen, Baron Walter von: *see* von
  Richthofen, Baron Walter
Rincon Kid: 212
Rogers, Jennie: 234–42
Rogers, Lottie: 208
Rooker, John: 4

Routt, Governor John L.: 268
Russell, Green: 3–4, 162
Russell, Lillian: 102

St. Charles, C. T.: 4–5
St. Mary's Academy: 184
Sand Creek Massacre: 162, 202
Sargent, M.: 83
Sayre, Hal: 57
Scamehorn, G. N.: 215
Seymour, Elva: 203
Sheedy, Dennis: 56
Sheridan, General Phil: 83
Sherman, General W. T.: 80
Silks, Mattie: 214, 234–35, 237–42
Skatara, the Mountain Chieftain (play):
  247
Skatterer, the Mountain Thief (play):
  247
Skyline Urban Renewal: 48
Smiley, Jerome C.: 150
Smith, Bascom: 212
Smith, Charlie: 207
Smith, Jefferson ("Soapy"): 142, 194,
  212
Smith, John: 4, 11
Smith, John W.: 83
Smoke, Davide: 7, 78
Snowshoe Itinerate: *see* Dyer, Father
  John
South Platte River: 3–4, 10, 13, 25, 228,
  277
Spalding, Bishop John: 147
Speer, Mayor Robert W.: 220, 224, 242
Stanley, Fay: 241
Steck, Judge Amos: 88
Steinberger, Captain A. B.: 247
Stockton, Bob: 217, 220
Stoiber, Lena: 68
Stone, Dr. J. S.: 79–80
Stranglers, The: 198
Sullivan, Dennis: 270
Sullivan, John L.: 134, 261
Sweet, Governor William E.: 70

Tabor, Augusta: 63, 258, 260
Tabor, Baby Doe: 61, 63–64, 85, 99,
  115–16, 240, 255–56, 258, 260
Tabor, H. A. W.: 63–64, 85, 94, 97, 99,
  115–16, 133–34, 150, 208, 254–56, 258,
  260
Tabor, Maxcy: 270

Tammen, Harry Heye: 61, 70–71, 98
Tammen, Mrs. Harry Heye: 61, 70
Tanner, Charley: 207
Tappan, Lewis N.: 120
Teats, Robert: 196
Thomas, Charles S.: 91
Thomson, Cort: 214–15
Thorne, Colonel Charles R.: 245–47
Thornton, James: 214, 216, 219
Thumb, Tom: 264
Trilby (painting): 220

University of Denver: 167, 179–84
University Park (Denver suburb): 26, 180
Uzzell, Parson Tom: 162

Vaillant, Father Joseph: *see* Machebeuf, Father Joseph P.
Vanderbilt, W. H.: 105
Vane, Cora: 208
Vinegar Hill: 228
von Richthofen, Baron Walter: 62

Waite, Governor Davis H.: 149
Wakely, Flora: 247
Wakely, George: 7, 247
Wakely, Louise: 247
Ward, Artemus: 251
Ward, Charley: 203
Washington, Mr. (American House porter): 83
Washington Park: 27
Wayne, David: 264
Wells, Kittie: 203
Wentworth, Charles: 87
Where is the Governor? (play): 250
Whispering Love (picture): 220
Whitsitt, Dick: 21
Wilde, Oscar: 96, 99, 106, 134, 151, 258
Williams, Andrew J.: 5–6
Williams, Mme: 203
Wilson, Clay: 212–13
Winner, Laura: 203
Wolcott, Edward O.: 99, 209, 268
Wootton, Richens L. (Uncle Dick): 6
Wyatt, Judge: 78

292